Fifth Avenue Princess to
American Dairy Queen

Deborah A. Benner

Fifth Avenue Princess to AMERICAN DAIRY QUEEN
Written by Deborah A. Benner
with Rebecca Rogers Nelson
Cover Photo and Layout by Erkel Associates

Murgolo Books

International Standard Book Number:

Printed in the United States of America

For information:
murgolobooks.com

Library of Congress Cataloging-in-Publication Data
LOC - 2011935560

ISBN 978-0-9837300-0-2

To the I AM of the I AMs—glory to God!

And to my husband, blessings to you, dear Arlin.

PART ONE

A WALK IN THE PARK

*Through the Word we are put together
and shaped up for the tasks God has for us.*
(2 Timothy 3:17, The Message)

Chapter 1

My Own Personal Burning Bush

Fall 1994, New York City

Walking down Madison Avenue one evening, on the way to work, the Holy Spirit interrupted my singing and said, "Are you ready to take a backseat? I am ready to bring your husband into your life, but you will have to take a backseat to him. Can you do that?" Of course I said I would have to think about it. After all, I was 36-years old, single and pretty happy with my life. I felt like I had been riding shotgun with God, all that time. So "backseat" sounded a bit, well... I'd think about it. I spent the rest of my walk to work analyzing the pros and cons of that question. After all, it was GOD talking, so I really did need to give it some thought.

Okay, just to get this out of the way, let me explain. When I say the Holy Spirit said something to me, it's not like I have a 1-800 direct dial-in to God or that I'm on the phone saying, "Hello God, ah, let's have a chat." Nor does He dial me up direct. God's voice is not audible to me, but it is recognizable, like recognizing a member of your family or a friend's voice. It is a distinct, familiar impression I get in my mind and in my heart. It took me a while to discern the difference between just talking to myself (God forbid, but that does happen!) and knowing it's Him. But now, it's pretty clear. I still have to check myself from time to time, but He always confirms, another lesson I've learned.

So, I was a struggling actor living in fabulous New York City, auditioning during the day, temping at night, which is where I was now headed. Life was finally enjoyable again, after a little detour the year before. It felt like I was getting myself back on track.

The previous fall, I sublet my New York apartment to a friend and headed to Los Angeles for "pilot season," the time of year when television networks do the bulk of their casting to gear up for new shows for the following season. Auditioning in L.A. was a bust for me, as it often was for many aspiring actors. Although la-la land was sunny and fun, I missed my life back in New York and headed home to the familiar hustle and bustle of The Big Apple. My friend had counted on being in my New York apartment longer, so I moved in with my youngest sister, Tex, who also lived in New York, just three blocks away from my place on East 78th Street between Fifth and Madison Avenues. I slept on the floor of her apartment on a futon and she slept in the loft. Though I missed my cozy apartment, I saved money on rent -- always important for a struggling actor. Plus, I still had the same neighborhood diner and Chinese laundry around the corner near Central Park, and the Metropolitan Museum one block away from "our" place on 81st and Madison.

That particular evening, I crossed over to walk through Central Park, the long way to get to my temp job, but I couldn't resist. Central Park any time of year is magnificent, but in the fall it transforms into a place of incredible beauty. This day the park was particularly so, but because of the husband bombshell question God had just dropped into my lap, my head was spinning. Even if I was ready "to take a backseat" to this unknown man; where was he? Better yet, who was he and how was I supposed to find him?

"God, you know, it must have been so much easier in the days of Moses to understand Your direction and what You were up to. I mean, how hard could it have been? You gave them a cloud by day and a fire by night. Yeah, I think I could have figured things out, that way, too. And, what about Moses, for Pete's sake, You spoke to him from a burning bush! Couldn't You have made my finding a husband clearer? I haven't had any burning bushes lately or ever for that matter. How the heck do You expect me to figure this out? What am I supposed to do? What's my part in all of this? How hard could it be to "get it" when you see a burning bush and hear a voice coming out of it, for crying out loud?!"

All of a sudden I looked up and directly in front of me was a huge, "big as Dallas" (as they say in Texas) bush that looked like it was on fire! Not literally, of course, but all its leaves had turned a vibrant yellow and golden color. It was cloudy that day, so it looked even more vivid against the backdrop of the grey sky. I stopped my muttering and laughed out loud. "Okay, okay, I get it; this is my burning bush, so now, what?"

Although never long enough, autumn is one of the best seasons to experience in New York City. The wind picks up, and the leaves dance with color as the city prepares for the excitement of the holidays. It's not just a tourist slogan; Christmas really is spectacular in New York. The Metropolitan has this amazing nativity scene set around a giant Christmas tree. The annual display features these incredible, handmade papier-mâché ornaments and biblical figurines that had been handed down through families for generations before being graciously donated to the museum. You need at least an hour to walk around the entire scene so you can take in all the details and beauty.

I also love the lighting of Park Avenue. On the second Sunday evening of Advent, everyone gathers at the Brick Presbyterian Church on 91st and Park to watch the Christmas lights come on. The lights start at one end and domino all the way down Park Avenue to the Metropolitan Life Building, it's so exciting! The crowd joins together singing Christmas carols and then, out of nowhere, a switch is hit and the lights turn the whole scene shimmery bright and the twinkle continues down the avenue. At the very end, a giant cross lights up on the side of the Met Life Building; it really is magnificent.

Of course, after doing this for years with "just the girls," even the bright holiday lights begin to dull, just a bit. True, I was happily single, but I did long for marriage and children, eventually. Honestly, I thought I would have been married by 30, at the latest. So now, at 36, I had begun to ask, a little more insistently lately, "God, where is my husband?"

So on that momentous evening, nearing the end of my walk, I sat down on a park bench and started counting. I'd been praying for my husband for about 17 years. Hello? Am I logged on? God's husband question pierced my heart. Yes, He was logged on. The question was, "Was I?"

Seventeen years was a long time to be praying and here, tonight, was my answer! AND I WAS HESITATING?

Yes, I was ready for my husband. And yes, gulp, I was ready to take a backseat. But what I was clearly not ready for was the roller coaster ride I was about to take to get to him.

Chapter 2

Where's My Husband?

When I got home from work that night, I poured a cup of hot tea, cozied up under a blanket on my futon, and opened my journals to remind myself of what God had spoken to me lately on the subject of marriage. I was curious, but I was also excited. If I was about to meet this guy, I wanted to look back to see if God had given me any hints on what to look for and I was not disappointed! Just the summer before, I had gone to Europe with Tex. As I was reading through my journals, I remembered God had indeed encouraged me in my time of waiting for His provision of a husband.

Tuesday, August 16, 1994, San Antonio, Texas

As the mountains surround Jerusalem, so the Lord surrounds His people both now and forevermore. (Psalm 125:2)

Lord, I believe in my heart I am already married and I thank You for Your gift. I give You thanks. Teach me how to thank You in a way that You find pleasing, that's enough to fill You up with delight.

"Deborah, if you will enjoy the gift that I have given you and find joy in him, this will gladden my heart and bring joy to Me. Don't work to the bone, child. Take everything in stride; be not anxious nor counting the days. Take today and just be here today."

Saturday, August 27, 1994, St. Marguerita, Italy, 8 p.m.

I'm now listening to some bells chiming from the hills. It is really beautiful here. Father, I thank You that Robert Gnocchi made a mistake when I called from St. Tropez, France, and Gnocchi said he had no space here. We came anyway and You opened a door for us to stay. How wonderful! While in St. Tropez, You really opened my eyes even more to my dependency on You. Everything revolved around how thin, beautiful, and rich a person was, all such fleeting things. Thank You for giving me the ability to constantly remind myself that You are the only reason for existing. And that my identity and my worth are hidden in You. Today I was reading in your Word about the man who was at the pool of Bethesda and how he was not expecting to be healed. He wasn't looking or asking for help. But after 30 years and reckoning himself dead to all of the possibilities of being healed, Jesus, You took the initiative with him and reached out to him and healed him. Yes, he had to start life over, and there must have been difficulties, but what spoke to me was that he did not have to do anything or perform to get You to have mercy on him. You just did.

Now, after praying and believing for a husband for so many years and trying to jump through every possible hoop for You, I realize I can just sit back and enjoy this fabulous vacation You have sent me on. And I come humbly before You and ask You once again, to have mercy and bring forth my husband. It's beyond me how You could do it or bring it to pass. But I know You can and You are able. Thank You! I have encountered the true source of living water—You, Jesus! Do please help me to be open to the unexpected ways You wish to act in my life. Thank You, Lord.

I had to chuckle at that last line. My walk in the park earlier that day proved, yet again, that God can act in unexpected ways. And the reality was, I didn't need to do anything. I simply needed to remain open to the unexpected.

Two months later, I learned that would be harder than I thought…

January 1995, Breakfast at my neighborhood diner, New York City

I had just finished browsing my favorite second-hand book shop when I stopped to grab a quick bite before heading home. As I munched on my English muffin, I began to have this sinking feeling, this knot in my stomach. I could tell God was moving and not only in me, but me physically from the city I so loved. I began to silently pray:

Father, I can sense there is a move coming in my life, a change away from Manhattan. Please, Father, do not move me out of New York City! I love this place. I love my apartment, the park, my friends, my church… But I can feel it; You are up to something… Please, Lord, I don't want to move! Thank You for this beautiful city, for the park, my apartment, friends, church, health, job, the beautiful skyline of buildings I see as I walk around the park…this sweatshirt I'm wearing…this English muffin I'm eating…

I went into my "thanksgiving" mode thinking that if I could just convince Him of how thankful I was, maybe, just maybe, He would change His mind and let me stay. And on and on I went, ad nauseam, as I was trying to con God into a change of plans. I sensed a move was coming—but where and why? I knew this feeling; I recognized it from one—and only one—other time in my life. That was when He moved me from Texas to New York City, January 1990.

December 1989, Miami, Florida

I was on holiday with my family. My siblings and parents flew in from all over and we were really having fun, basking in the sun, hanging out, and of course enjoying my mom's cooking. We are Italian, we live for good food and love to eat; plus meal time is the one time when we all sit around together and can dig into some real conversation.

My sister Tex had moved to New York City two years before; after her college graduation in 1987. Every chance she got, she begged me to move there as well. I usually just shook my head and walked away. But this night, across the dinner table, she must have read something different in my facial expression that gave her hope. She got really excited and teased me by singing, "You're moving to New York, you're moving to New York!"

I dropped my fork and shot back at her, "No, I am not!" "I have my work and my house and—"

But, my father interrupted in his still lingering New York accent, "You should go. Take a couple of months, see what it's like. You've worked hard. You deserve a little break."

As my dad spoke, I realized I was a bit tired. Maybe I did need a little… sabbatical.

I didn't say anything to Tex, maybe because of all her teasing. But on the plane ride back to Texas, after our family vacation, I began to justify the idea of a New York City visit.

During the past few years, I had been on the fast track starting my own business. Things were going well. I was selling Mary Kay – doesn't everyone do the Mary Kay thing at least once in their lifetime? Well, in Texas, you do. I actually did makeovers and makeup artistry work for my customers and I had the idea of working with ladies in groups. It was fun for them and better for my business. Plus, I wasn't into the facial Door-to-door thing. So, I put together fashion shows at a popular Italian restaurant, created a menu with a great lunch, went to major businesses with lots of secretaries and sold packages that included gift certificates for Mary Kay products.

I pitched the idea as a unique gift for the hard-working women in their company: a delightful break on Secretary Day. "What an amazing treat to be honored at a wonderful luncheon in a great restaurant complete with exquisite food and a fantastic fashion show." I booked the models and called the TV and radio stations. Bingo! I had instant press and was in business. It was great!

Word spread and my business grew. Soon, I had my own three-bedroom home with a small guesthouse in the back, a nice car, and my beautiful white German shepherd. I wasn't going anywhere; or, so I thought.

Back then I had the same feeling I had that morning in the diner while eating my English muffin. And, true to myself, I began to "discuss" this with God.

Lord, I am not moving to New York City. I have a home, a dog, and work in San Antonio. I'm over 30, and I am not starting over in a new place, especially New York City and single! I mean, come on! I would move if I were married, but not single. Who am I going to meet in New York City? Not happening, God. I'll go to visit Tex for a couple of months and then that's it. I'm coming back to Texas.

Thinking I wasn't staying long, I took one suitcase of clothing and the giant box mom had packed for Tex's apartment. I left a fully furnished, three-bedroom home, my beautiful dog Zeik, my car, and my personal belongings. Looking out the window as my plane was landing at La Guardia Airport, I had that feeling: "Lord, I'm not ever going back home again, am I?"

His short answer arrived in my heart, "New York City, there you go!"

As soon as I got off the plane and my feet hit the ground, something inside felt like I had just returned home after a long stay away. It was unexplainable. "This is home now," I heard in my heart.

I never did return for my house, my belongings, or Zeik. My parents, at my request, gave away my stuff, sold the house, and gave away the car. My sweet dog Zeik went to live with my handyman, Joe, who adored him. Joe took him on all of his jobs and Zeik was never happier.

Coming to New York meant starting all over again. Amazingly, I was thrilled! I moved into my sister's tiny one-bedroom, second-floor apartment on East 74th and Madison Avenue above an awesome deli called Frazier Morris. Tucked inside an old Vanderbilt building with the entrance on 74th Street, we walked up crooked stairs that looked and felt as if they were about to fall over. But it was a corner apartment with windows on Madison and 74th. Fabiola!

I lived off the adrenaline of my new surroundings; I mean the town never sleeps. In fact, the first two weeks, I couldn't sleep. Traffic was so intense down Madison Avenue. It went on and on every night until about 10 p.m. Then at 12 a.m., after a brief two—hour 'cat nap,' I would be awakened by this hideous beeping noise a truck makes when it goes into reverse: Beep, beep, beep! It was the trash man paying us his nightly visit. That was followed by the clop-clop-clopping of policemen on horseback. How did anyone ever get any rest around here?!

In spite of city life adjustments, I was falling in love with this huge, fast-paced metropolis; it was becoming home. I slept on the couch for a few days until I could purchase a single bed, but the bedroom wasn't quite wide enough for two single beds. We had to walk sideways between our two beds nestled eight inches apart! Closeness: New-York style. I wasn't complaining. I was learning the ropes of big city life.

Through all this change, I became increasingly aware of my heart's desire to be married. I had just turned 31, and, like most gals my age, I longed for that soul mate, the one with whom I would share all my secrets, joys, dreams, concerns, doubts, fears…and my heart. I had been praying since I became a believer in 1978 for the man God had chosen for me. In the late 1980s, I relinquished my right to choose for myself. I had made a lot of wrong choices in my 20s and was tired of wasting time and emotional energy. I wanted God to choose for me.

Okay, full disclosure time. Here's the reason I say, "I relinquished my rights to choose for myself…" I was married for a brief time in the mid-80s. I was 27, teaching high school Spanish and earning a meager $18K a year. I was burning out fast. My sister Tex encouraged me to meet her friend, the owner of the most successful Mexican restaurant in San Antonio, Texas, and Tex told me I would make more money waiting tables than I ever could by teaching. Making a change and making more money sounded great. There was only one issue: most of the waiters were male, and they didn't hire females as a general rule. However, Tex made a call, I met the owner, and I was hired. I loved it! Tex was right; I was raking in the tips and earning much more than teaching.

About two weeks into the job I met a very handsome waiter, a Tom Selleck look-alike from Mexico, with a beautiful accent. My head was turned. He was a prince of a fellow; not only was he dashing, but he had an incredible work ethic. But his special ability was knowing how to make a woman feel like a queen. He wooed, and I fell. After our first lunch together I went home and a word came to me "The wolves are coming." I knew instantly that this was an Isaiah 33 deal. He was my Ishmael and not an Isaac. But like Sarah, I was tired of waiting and didn't trust God to come through on His end.

We "fell in love" and had a quick Justice of the Peace ceremony. Immediately afterwards, I knew I'd made a mistake. The marriage was annulled within months. He was a wonderful man who treated me like a queen. My family adored him, and yet, from the bottom of my soul, I knew marrying him was wrong for me. When I first met him, I knew in my gut that I was not to start seeing him. I sensed the Holy Spirit saying, "He's not the one I have for you, not yet. Just wait." I remembered the warning He had given me, but I plowed ahead, ignoring it just the same. In the end, I realized I just could not continue the marriage. Because of my clear disobedience, I struggled with the consequences of my actions more than at any other time in my life. The most painful part was how much I hurt him. After the annulment, he returned to Mexico, and I took a nanny job in Palm Beach. I couldn't stay in San Antonio; it was too painful.

From that time on, I knew the man/husband issue was up to God. I could not be trusted to make the right decision, and I wasn't about to make a move again without His clear directive. But I could pray! And I did, often.

"God, You brought Eve to Adam, Sarah to Abraham, and Rebecca to Isaac. You say You are not a respecter of persons. So, I am asking You to do for me what You did for them—to put me before my husband, to bring me to him. And I want him to be a man so full of love for You that he hears Your voice. That when You put me before him, he can hear You say, 'That's her' and I can hear You say to me, 'That's him.'"

He does ask us to make all our requests known to Him, doesn't He?

But now, living in NYC, a hustling, bustling town packed with millions of people everywhere, all I could ask was, "Car 54, where are you?!" And how will I know him when I see him? God was about to answer that question in the most unimaginable way…

Chapter 3

The Audition

February 1995, Third Avenue, New York

I was wandering down Third Avenue one afternoon buying my fruit for the day from the local stands when I felt the Holy Spirit say, "Buy *Backstage.*" *Backstage* is a newspaper for actors and lists all kinds of auditions: singing, stage, television, and film. As usual, I had to question the Holy Spirit on this one because I was living on a $10-a-day food budget, and the paper cost $2.50! Finally, I gave in and said, "Fine, it's Your money and if You want to waste $2.50 on a dumb newspaper, okay!" I had already learned that almost every audition offered through this paper turned out to be for a script I could not – in good conscience – even read, much less perform.

While munching on my just-bought apple, I began flipping through the paper. My eyes were immediately drawn to a heading in the theater section: GOSPEL SINGING. Well, I love to sing gospel music, so I read on. The audition listed was for a play simply called Noah. There were eight lead roles for actors. The only catch was that the play was in Lancaster, Pennsylvania.

Well, I always did want to experience the Amish, I thought. Perhaps I'll go for it. But… Ugh! It's in a dumb Christian theatre, probably a third-rate, unprofessional, rinky-dink, dowdy place. Oh well, it's a job that seems to pay well. I need to get my Actor's Equity Card, could use the money… Hmm… Could be like a six-month sabbatical and I want out of New York City for the summer. I loved the city, but the summer really was brutal; all that concrete and no escape. I was too broke to do weekend retreats to the Hamptons or Fire Island so this seemed like a nice option. If I booked the Noah gig, I could have my own little 'low-income' summer retreat, rent a cute, modest place, see a little grass and be neighbors with some cows; oh, the irony.

Okay Lord, I decided if they call then I will go to the audition. I sent in my head shot and resume and within two days I got a call. The audition was the following week.

Meanwhile, I called my friend Becky, who was also an actor, to tell her about the audition and ask if she knew anything about it. She said she knew of another actor from our church who was given an audition for the same play. She suggested the two of us travel down together. So, we contacted each other and found four other girls going down for the first audition. Six girls crammed into a little two-door car—your basic ride from hell!

When we arrived, I was blown away, excited, and humbled, all at the same time. The "rinky-dink" Christian theatre I had envisioned was a $15 million dollar complex with a 1,200-seat auditorium and a 300-foot surround stage. The sets alone cost over $2 million dollars. For the second act, they built the inside of the ark. It was 40 feet high and 300 feet in diameter! Over 200 actors from all over the U.S. were said to have auditioned for this play. *Wow!* This was a much bigger deal than I thought. Now I really wanted the job!

Of course, I repented for my elitist and judgmental attitude and began to beg God for help as I stumbled through practice for one of the dance numbers. There were four parts to the audition: voice, cold read, personal interview (to assess where the actors were, spiritually) and… then there was dance. I could sing, I could read and I loved God, but dance – God help me on that one! Thankfully, he did and finally the audition process was over.

Man, was I tired. We drove for four hours, got a $120 speeding ticket, auditioned, and now we were on our way back to New York. We returned at 5 a.m.—absolutely exhausted—but the ride back was much better; only three of us in a two-door rental car. Praise Jesus, hallelujah!

One month later, callbacks came. I was the only one out of our group given a second audition. Again, I was humbled. The gals I had traveled with were seasoned and very talented. I knew God had gifted me, too, but why was I the only one called? I had to wonder, "Are you up to something, God?"

I returned in March for the callbacks. Two days later, I was offered a swing shift to one of the lead roles. That means, I was guaranteed full pay, a set number of performances and I had to commit to six months in Podunk Pennsylvania. Just a side note, the news of my booking came on the heels of my walk in Central Park when I got the "you're about to meet your husband, can you take a backseat" love bomb and when I began *fervently* praising the Lord and thanking Him for bringing me to New York City six years earlier, telling Him how much I loved living here and never wanted to leave. It was also when I felt deep down in my spirit a change coming—a move away from the city.

I, however, was in denial—and as the saying goes, 'that ain't no river in Egypt!' "Lord, *please* don't permanently take me out of New York City! For the summer, fine, but not forever; I love my life here!" Even if I was living on a ten-dollar-a-day budget, I was finally in my own fabulous rent-controlled studio apartment on East 78th Street, between Fifth and Madison. It was one block from the Metropolitan Museum of Art, and Central Park was my backyard! What more could I ask for?

The play was to run for six months including rehearsals, starting in April, ending in October. One night before I went to bed, I prayed, "Lord, do I need to move my furniture and take all my clothes, or what?"

That same morning, the Holy Spirit woke me up at 5 a.m., "Don't even take two tunics, just take one." He gave me a vision of a beautiful little house totally furnished on a wide expanse of land. I knew that this meant to only take the clothes I would need and leave everything else.

"But Lord, who will rent me a furnished house for six months, and in the middle of the year? What about my place?" As God would have it, Becky had recently introduced me to Karri, a new friend of hers from church who had just relocated from L.A. Conveniently enough; she was looking for a temporary place for the next six months! Karri sublet my apartment.

Two weeks before I was to be in Lancaster to start rehearsals, I finally decided I'd better go and look for a place to live. Karri and I had become friends, and since she was anxious to move into my place, she was more than happy to help me find a place in Lancaster as soon as possible!

We rented a car—another miracle. Rental cars in New York City on the weekends went for more than $100 a day, if you could find one. I befriended one of the assistants at my temp job whose father knew someone with a car rental business in Westchester. He offered me a rental car for a reduced rate of $25 per day! When Karri and I went to pick up the car on Friday afternoon, the reservationist had a funny look on her face.

"No, no, that can't be right," she said. She continued to punch the keys on her computer. When she realized what she was reading was correct, she looked up at us with an inquisitive smile crossing her face, "Who do you know that you got this rate?"

"God," I wanted to say, but, she would have thought I was nuts. So, I opted to just smile and take the keys. We set out with a map, water bottles, and overnight bags. We were on a mission to find the house God had given me in my vision.

We arrived in Strasburg, Pennsylvania and rented a hotel room next to the theatre. Fortunately, the theatre administration secretary, Helen, had taken a liking to me over the phone. Although we had never met in person and had only spoken over the phone a few times, we seemed to have a similar sense of humor and our personalities just clicked. Later she told me as soon as she saw my headshot, she had a feeling that I would be coming to work there.

Helen met us at check-in. She had her car packed with an ice chest full of drinks and snacks and was ready to take us driving around to find a place for me to live. I was feeling particularly blessed at that moment.

We made a right turn out of the theatre and came to a light at the corner. I noticed a man putting up a sign that read FOR RENT for an apartment on Main Street, in historic Strasburg.

Yuk! "This was not the cute place I had envisioned..." Knowing how hard it was to find anything that close to the theatre, Helen suggested I put my name on the list as a backup plan, in case we didn't find anything else. Begrudgingly, I agreed. She really was looking out for me; she knew I didn't have transportation and this was within walking distance to the theatre and all of my rehearsals.

She drove us around all day to every apartment complex she could think of and a few small rental houses too. I became more discouraged as the day wore on. We stopped at a furniture rental place after Helen suggested an unfurnished apartment.

I said," But Helen! The Lord has shown me a little house completely furnished on lots of land and that's what I'm looking for. That's what I want!" She looked at me as if I was an alien who had just landed and I didn't quite have a full grasp of the lay of the land. In other words, she must have thought…*nut job!*

At the furniture rental place, we ran into another actress named Joyce, who was cast to play the role of Mrs. Noah. Joyce had come from Pittsburgh to look for a place to live. We remembered each other from the auditions a month earlier and congratulated each other for booking the gig. She had found a place in Landisville, wherever that was, but she was still looking for something closer. We wished each other luck on finding accommodations and agreed to have coffee when we were both back in town for rehearsals. But honestly, at this point I was thinking, "There's no way I'm going to stay and take this job. I mean, if I have to leave New York City for six months and move to cow country, it had better be for a place with character and charm and romance, not some cheesy apartment complex!"

Helen said she had one more place to show me, she'd just remembered, but it was 30-minutes by car from the theatre. By now it was 4 p.m. and I was ready to go back home to New York City and forget the whole thing. Karri was beginning to worry. Her apartment sublet was contingent on me finding a place that made me happy in Lancaster. I wasn't finding a place and neither one of us were happy. She said, "Deb, let's just go look at the place, we're here, what could it hurt?" She was right.

So we all climbed back in the car and drove to a one-light town called Landisville. We pulled into a gated area named The Camp Woods located on 25 acres of beautiful land with about 20 of the cutest little storybook cottages I had ever seen. We came around the bend, slowing down as we approached a two-story cottage that looked like Hansel and Gretel's place; I'm not kidding. The shutters almost looked like they had been made with fluffy white frosting and peppermint candies!

I jumped out of the car before Helen could slow to a stop. I ran over to the porch and jumped up and down screaming, "This is it! This is the house! This is the house God gave me in my vision!" Helen and Karri exchanged glances, then we all began laughing.

I boldly knocked on the door, several times; no one was home. I looked over to Karri as I timidly tried the knob. She nodded as I turned the knob, and the door opened! Karri, Helen, and I snuck in and looked around. Helen assured us it would be okay, she knew the landlords, and after all, she was their neighbor!

The house was completely furnished in beautiful antiques. There was a kitchen, a formal living room and dining room, complete with a china cabinet full of china and crystal. There was even a laundry room! This was important, because the last thing I needed was to carry my laundry back and forth to town after a long day of rehearsal. Did I say rehearsal?! I guess I was still considering the idea of staying and doing the show!

I dashed upstairs where I found two beautifully decorated bedrooms, a cozy sitting room, and a full bath. It was charming, had character; it was lovely—and it was *home!*

Smiling, I turned to Helen. She laughed, shook her head, and quickly pulled out her cell and started dialing. The owner, Yvonne, ran a bed and breakfast named Green Acres. We kept getting the answering machine. It played the theme song from the TV series of the same name. In a country twang, the lyrics included, "Farm living is the life for me!" Little did I know how prophetic that phone message would be.

When we got back to the hotel we finally reached Yvonne! Sadly, she informed us that Joyce (the woman playing Mrs. Noah who I had just run into earlier that day) had rented the house back in February! Yvonne was apologetic, but Joyce had put down the first month's rent; it was a done deal. Joyce and her husband had not seen the place yet, but she was coming the next day.

I was confused. I knew that this was the house God had for me. How could I have gotten it so wrong? I was so disappointed!

And poor Yvonne was on the other end of my 'disappointment' as my voice continued to crescendo into the phone, "You don't understand! This is the house I saw in a vision from the Lord—He showed me where I was going to live and I really believe this is my house!" Silence on the other end of the line. I knew what she was thinking: "whack job!"

How God has tolerated my tantrums from time to time, I wonder...; although I certainly don't think He's running all over heaven pulling out His hair and screaming, "Oh no! Oh no! She's going to mess up My plans!" More like, "Uh-huh... Watch this, guys, watch what she does now..." in His calm sovereignty while smiling at the heavenly hosts.

Karri and I went out for the evening; she sipped wine while I vented. We returned to the hotel late that night only to find that we had been locked out of our room. Our room key, for some reason, didn't work. Beyond annoyed, I stomped down the stairs to the lobby, cursing under my breath and guess who just happened to be standing at the front desk? Joyce's husband, Frank! They were staying at the *same* hotel; how oddly coincidental. *Okay, let's just call it what it is: "Hello, God!"*

Frank asked me what living arrangements I had found. I quickly told him about the apartment in Strasburg and avoided eye contact... or mentioning the cottage. I knew he and Joyce had not been to see it yet, and if I told him how adorable it was, they would take it for sure. Maybe, just *maybe* if I played it right, I might still have a shot. Even though they had put a deposit on the cottage back in February, sight unseen, they still wanted to check out options closer to the theatre. My plan was to dissuade them from even going to see the place. I went on the offensive. I began to talk up the town and how great it was going to be to be so close to the theatre. "It will almost feel like living in New York," I said with a very forced smile.

Then he interrogated me. "I heard you went to see the cottage we rented. (Uh-oh) What did it look like? Could you see anything? How many bedrooms did it have?"

What was this, the third degree? I evaded his questions and mumbled, "Yes we saw it, but nobody was there to let us in." I quickly grabbed the key from the front desk gal and headed back to the stairs. I heard him call after me, "Well," he said. "Did you look through the windows? Was it cute? How was it furnished?" What man ever cares about how a place is furnished or how cute it is? Especially since his wife was making the move and he was staying in

Pittsburgh with their house and his job! I turned back to him and said, a little louder than I had planned, "Yeah, it looked cute!"

I turned and quickly ran up the stairs to my room, I wanted out of there. I shoved the key in the door, pushed Karri in the room, and slammed the door behind us. Karri looked at me intently and I instantly felt guilty.

God was testing me through this man to see if I would be willing to give up the house and be completely honest about how fabulous it was. No, I wasn't. I failed— capital F!

That night I couldn't sleep. I paced the floor most of the night because the conviction of my selfish attitude was heavy on my heart. When I did lie down, I just tossed and turned. Karri, on the other hand, slept *wonderfully.*

Finally, it was morning. At 7 a.m., I sat up in bed, read my Bible, and talked to God. He led me to Philippians 2:1–4: "If you have any encouragement from being united with Christ, if any comfort from His love, if any fellowship with the Spirit, if any tenderness and compassion, then make My joy complete by being like-minded, having the same love, being one in spirit and purpose. Do *nothing* out of vain conceit, but in humility consider *others* better than you. Each of you should look not only to your own interests, *but also to the interests of others.*" In His profound, gentle way, He nailed me. My vision was clear; I had to tell Joyce about the house and be willing to lose it.

Immediately, I threw off the covers and hurried down to the lobby, in my silk pajamas and pink fuzzy slippers. I asked the front desk woman, who was looking at me in my pj's, what room Joyce was in. She began politely declining the information explaining customer confidentiality when Frank came to the lobby and saw me. He practically ran over to me and said, "We've been trying to call your room all morning! Joyce wants to talk to you."

"Good," I sighed, "I need to talk to her too."

Frank rang their room from the lobby and Joyce came down. I barely gave her a chance to sit down as I spilled the whole story of how I had not only seen the house, but I walked all through it. I gave her full descriptive details of how adorable and perfect it was. Then I confessed I secretly wanted the cottage and I didn't want her to know how great it was because once she saw it she wouldn't want to give it up. She couldn't get a word in edgewise, as I kept verbally tripping all over myself, apologizing and telling her what a splendid summer she was going to have in that perfect little cottage.

Then, she began laughing. I stopped mid-sentence, which made her laugh even harder. I asked her what was so funny. Joyce was laughing so hard, she couldn't talk, so I kept on with my apology. Finally, she began waving her hands as if trying to flag down a train; I finally became quiet. She sighed deeply with a smile on her face, "Good! It's yours! I couldn't sleep all night because I want that apartment you have on hold in Strasburg. That's where I want to live -- on Main Street!" My mouth dropped open. We both reached for each other at the same time in a relieved hug. Joyce was as happy as I was. She was getting exactly what she wanted and I was getting what I was sure God had for me; only I had to be willing to give it up.

What a *miracle!* God had that house on hold for me since February! He knew all along where I was going to live—even as I was digging my heels into New York City, refusing to go look for a place to stay. And even though I had waited until the last minute to go to Lancaster, by His grace, I was right on time. Amazing how He can work with our imperfections, keeping us on the path He has for us, even if we fight it. God is so good, even though I am clearly sometimes so…not! I could only imagine Him sitting in heaven with the heavenly hosts, smiling with an "I told you so!" look on His face. Of course, that's my stereotypical Italian Mother version of God. I'm sure He's much more gracious than that!

The next morning, I called Yvonne, explained the turn of events, and she rented me the cottage. However, I did have one minor problem. The theatre was in Strasburg, a 30-minute drive from the cottage in Landisville, and I had no car.

"No problem," Yvonne said. "My husband buys and sells used cars. Just tell me how much you can afford, and he'll have a car ready for you when you get here." Great, what could be easier than that? But my temp job was soon ending. I had just enough to survive before my trip down to Lancaster. I had no extra money for a car.

As I had learned from the cottage drama, God already has the situation figured out. All I really need to do is spend time with Him in prayer, *thanking Him in advance* for what He is about to do. So it was back to the prayer closet for me. God wanted me in Lancaster, so I knew He would figure out transportation once I got there. I just wasn't quite sure how the money for that transportation would materialize. "O ye of little faith," I scolded myself. Just give me some sandals and call me an Israelite! Didn't I just see him part the Red Sea last week? Now I doubted all over again. I repented; trust grew.

One week later, my income tax return check came – $1000. I could now afford a very inexpensive but dependable car. *Yippee!* Right on time!

The next hurdle was how to get to Lancaster from New York City with all my stuff. It was just a few personal items and some clothes, but I had to get it there, and of course, I was still on my very tight budget. A good friend of mine, Heidi, had just decided to quit her job and travel around the country for six months taking the scenic route back home to Texas. Jokingly, I mentioned to her that Lancaster is pretty scenic this time of year. She took me seriously, looked it up on the map, and decided it would be a fun detour on her trip. Heidi called me all chatty about the Amish country and how fun it was going to be. She was so sweet, acting as if I was doing her the favor! She had just leased a Jeep Cherokee and was ready for an adventure! *Wow, God! You really do supply every need. You decide where you want me and you work out the details…and pay the way!*

Just call me a slow learner. Back at my apartment in New York City, I was in major denial again, refusing to pack. How could I be in denial, after all that had just happened? Nevertheless, I was having panic attacks over the thought of leaving my apartment. I was afraid I was losing control and would never make it back to my safe New York City haven. I remembered the feeling I had that day in January while walking in the park, this felt *permanent*, and I was scared.

The night before I was to leave for the next six months, Karri, who had sublet my apartment, brought over a few of her things. She looked around at the chaos and decided to help me pack. She kept clearing shelves, packing all my family pictures in my suitcase. When she turned around to get more things, I would sneak over to the suitcase and quickly snatch them up and put them back. Karri pulled clothes out of my closet and drawers and put them in the suitcase. She would carefully wrap my personal items and place them snugly in the suitcase. As soon as she would put them in, I would trail behind her and pull them out, like an Abbott and Costello routine.

When she finally caught on to what I was doing, she looked at me sideways. I sweetly smiled and insisted I only needed a few things because, after all, I was only going to be gone for six months. Bottom line: I just didn't believe God could have anything better for me anywhere else than what I had here. *I loved New York City!* Karri thrust out her hand and demanded the family photo I was attempting to put back on the shelf. With a heavy sigh, I relinquished and watched, pensively, as she wrapped it back up and put it in my suitcase.

I knew I was acting crazy, but I couldn't help myself. I was afraid I would never return to New York. Finally, I gave in; God had made it beyond clear what I was to do. Now, it was my turn to let go, trust, and try to enjoy the ride.

The next morning, Heidi pulled up in front of my place on 78th Street. Karri put my suitcase in the back of the jeep and firmly closed the door. She looked me in the eyes and gently said, "You really are doing the right thing." She gave me a long hug goodbye and then waited until she saw Heidi's jeep pull away before she went back inside my— I mean her apartment. I'm sure she wanted to make sure I was really going!

By the somber expression on my face, Heidi could tell I was less than enthusiastic about my move. We drove in silence for a bit, but as we crossed over the George Washington Bridge and began to pull away from the city, something began to happen; a glint of excitement began to rise up in me. My heart actually started to feel lighter, as if I really was embarking upon an adventure. Of course, I couldn't know how this was going to all play out; I had to have complete trust in God.

Heidi began to joke and talk about old times, I smiled, remembering. Soon, we were both laughing and really enjoying the drive. The weather was spectacular and the countryside was beautiful, a perfect start to our trip. We chatted about where in life we thought we were headed and what God was doing in each of our lives. It ended up being a beautiful drive and a lot of fun.

After what seemed a short time, we arrived at The Camp Woods. Heidi marveled at how pretty the whole area was, and we both couldn't wait to get to the cottage.

As we drove around the bend, we saw the cutest guy walking down the road. Heidi said, "Hmm… he's adorable. Looks like this could be an interesting summer after all!" I slapped her arm playfully. Following right behind him, however, were his wife and two small sons. She laughed and said, "Cute and taken." "Just like New York," I chimed in. We both got a laugh out of that one.

Her next comment was, "Oh, Deborah, I can just see it now. You're going to meet a dairy farmer, get married, and live here the rest of your life. You're never going back to New York City!" Her words splashed on me like cold water, and my adventurous mood was gone. As she laughed, I steamed and shouted, "Shut up! I'm not moving here or marrying a dairy farmer! My husband is not within 100 miles of this place! I'm sure of it."

"Okay, okay, just a joke," Heidi said, lightly. I calmed down, but there was something in her words that lingered. A shiver went up my spine, as I pictured myself in overalls, smiling with a milk mustache. I couldn't shake the image. But at the same time, my heart leapt with new hope. The thought of falling in love and making a place like this home felt strangely… truthful.

As we unloaded, Yvonne came over to greet us. She was smiling, very friendly, and so accommodating. She treated us like family. She sent us to eat dinner at a homey restaurant in Mount Joy. It was a local hangout, and Heidi and I couldn't help but stare as some of the patrons came in, 'right off the farm.' These folks weren't kidding around. They walked, talked, and I guessed, ate cows. Dairy farming was their livelihood; they were the real deal. These folks seemed very cordial, but I could only imagine what they were thinking about us. I was dressed in my animal-print vest and black turtleneck and Heidi was wearing tight jeans and high heels. I couldn't help but giggle at the stark contrast. We stood out like a couple of city slickers who'd lost our way from Hershey Park or the Amish country tour.

The next day was Sunday. We had a wonderful country breakfast in my new kitchen. But then Heidi had to get on the road. We had our tearful, girly goodbyes. When she left, I suddenly felt very alone. I tried to busy myself unpacking my clothes, putting out my family pictures, fluffing up pillows and arranging things to make them feel like home. That took about 45 minutes. I sat down on the couch and realized how quiet it was. I knew no one well enough to invite over and I had no TV, which was okay because I rarely watched television, but it would have been nice to have some movement or sound in the room.

"Okay, God, it's just You and me. I'll look at this like a six-month time of spiritual rejuvenation." I was giving my own pep talk. Yes, I knew God was listening, but I was really trying to convince myself more than anyone else. I put on some praise music and forced myself to sit back on the couch. It was still warm enough for the windows to be open, and I felt the cool breeze blow through my hair. I finally felt my shoulders drop as I began to sing with the music. The spirit was with me, I could feel His peace in the room and I really did begin to feel rejuvenated.

Chapter 4

The Show Must Go On!

On Monday I went to the theatre for the first rehearsal, the start of a grueling eight-week schedule. We had dance rehearsals, voice lessons, gymnastics, juggling, roping (yes, roping,) and more. Plus, we practiced how to move on stage with large props and live animals. It really was a zoo – or in this case, an ark. We were preparing to open on June 27th and to begin performing 12 two-and-a-half-hour shows a week. Not only was it an exhausting eight weeks of rehearsals, but the show schedule itself was a killer. All the shows sold out before we even opened. If the schedule was to be followed exactly, and we were assured it would be, we would end up performing for 18,000 people a week.

I get tired just repeating it, but at the time, I wasn't tired at all. Just the opposite: I began to be energized by the schedule, anxious to learn the next new thing and giddy with what was becoming 'the norm' in my life—hanging out with huge giraffes and all! Aside from all the prep work and rehearsing for the play, I had begun taking horseback riding lessons (actually, jumping lessons) at a local stable. My older sister Jean and I used to show horses when we were kids, and I always wanted to get back to riding. My breaks from the theatre were few and far between, but riding was relaxing for me, so I welcomed the opportunity.

I was cooling down my horse one day after my lesson, and as I walked through a beautiful pasture, I stopped. I took in the extensive surrounding farmland dotted by cows slowly grazing across pastures, enclosed by beautiful storybook white picket fences. I had an epiphany: I just loved my life! I felt like I was living in a dream. Here I was, living in the most beautiful spot, in a gingerbread cottage, doing what I loved to do, and getting paid for it!

Back at the cottage, I finished a light dinner, and then climbed into a hot bubble bath to sooth my aching muscles. As I lay back, soaking by candlelight, I asked, "God, how could it get any better? And why are You so good to me?" In the bubbly silence, I began to really ponder that question and to *thank* Him for what was happening in my life at that moment. I truly felt like I was reaping the benefits of my obedience, albeit kicking and screaming, to leave New York City and come to this tiny little town in Pennsylvania. I reflected that it's not always easy to obey, but as a result, trust in His ways was growing! Wonder of wonders, obedience was paying off and I really did not want to let my fear or lack of trust get in the way again. So, I wrote in my journal about it.

Wednesday May 3 1995

My body is extremely sore today from all the gymnastics, etc., but I have to explore this question: Do I sometimes allow my "self" to get in the way of God's plan and design? Yes. Many times I do, because I can't see the whole plan, so I get scared. Or, I presume the future and then get upset when it doesn't come to pass the way I expect. Have I thought of myself way too much? Yes. Because I have thought about "fame" as an actress in the secular world and that I'm giving that up for this, this "Christian" production. It was ridiculous to not give in to God with joy at His plans for my life—and to trust I am not missing anything. What is His compassion? That He chooses me! He chooses to love me and to use me. Lord, help me to receive Your love, to be open to You!

Now, I was on to something! Doing things my way was okay, but doing things in complete abandonment to God's way – that was amazing! Of course, the minute I began to feel confident in this new realization, the enemy got busy trying to shake my confidence.

It was the end of the first week of rehearsals and all was going great until I was injured doing a gymnastics stunt. I went to the doctor, who declared I had to be off my knee for three weeks. Now, Christian or not, the show must go on, and to miss three weeks out of an eight week rehearsal schedule was just unacceptable. The director threatened to let me go. He said if I couldn't be on stage for blocking, then he'd have to replace me and I'd be out of a job. That put me in a small state of shock, needless to say. After everything that had happened to get me there, I was scared I would be fired for a work-related injury and my journey cut short.

Of course, I took matters into my own hands. I went back home to the cottage that day and immediately called Karri to tell her my predicament. I told her I might be returning to New York a little earlier than I had planned.

"You promised me six months in your apartment, Deborah. I'm sorry things aren't working out for you there, but I'm going to keep you to your word. I've moved all my stuff in and am counting on being here for the full six months."

She was right. Besides, I had just signed a six-month lease myself and bought a car. My knee was throbbing, my mind was racing. What was I going to do?

Friday, May 5, 1995

Today after gymnastics I went home and cried and cried. I have severely hurt my knee and can barely walk. I feel so terrible, incapacitated, and alone. I don't like this "personal stretching." It's painful. My fears are not being able to exercise and not being able to shed excess weight. I'll never amount to anything if I can't be in the physical shape I need to; I must be thin and healthy and look my best. These are my thoughts and so many more. Film and TV are so much easier to do. God, why have You brought me here? I can't feel any more of a failure than I do today. And for what? They have put so much money into this production. I felt terrible when they prayed over me the other night. They prayed extensively over each person—but hardly prayed over me. They only thanked God for the circumstances that brought me here, that You would fill me with Your knowledge. They thanked You for my calling and that I would step into what You have for me. I was saddened because I felt left out. I feel increasingly less and less a part of the group and more and more alienated. You're only going to give me what I need when I need it. You're not going to give me the whole picture. I have to tell myself not to give in to the enemy—to hold on, because it's all true— everything you've said, God, has happened. I know your plan will come to pass. What You spoke will happen.

Finally I said to the Lord, "Okay, if they fire me, they fire me. I know you're in this, too. I'll look for a job in a grocery store or restaurant or something. I'm committed here for six months and I'll just tough it out."

To my utter amazement, the theatre agreed to keep me on. I was determined to not let them down. I watched every rehearsal, wrote down my blocking and walked through the routines as best I could. I was also diligent with my physical therapy for my knee and gradually it began to feel better. My strength returned, as did my participation level with rehearsals. I could feel the cast gaining confidence in me, and truly, I did not want to disappoint anyone. Eventually my knee healed. By my first scheduled performance, my knee was back to normal. Because of all the extra workouts, I was in the best shape in years. I felt physically fortified, confident and ready for anything.

I don't think we'll ever know for sure God's purpose for the things that happen in our lives until we get to Heaven. However, maybe my injury and recovery were about learning to overcome, to persevere, even when the goal seemed unattainable. Perseverance would be a trait I would need again, in the very near future.

Chapter 5

Everyone's Related to Yvonne

During my first few weeks in Lancaster, everyone I met seemed to be related to Yvonne. The carpenter she hired to work on the cottage was her brother-in-law; my neighbor (the cute guy with the wife and two kids) was her nephew, and the young woman I met at Yvonne's bed and breakfast one day was her niece. The woman who was helping Yvonne prepare the 125th anniversary party for The Camp Woods was her sister-in-law, and Yvonne's son was married to the daughter of the theater's owner.

Yvonne also introduced me to her daughter, Barb. Yvonne thought we might have some things in common since we were both about the same age and both single. All of her relatives were wonderful and open to me, but meeting Barb changed my life.

Generally the theatre gave us Sundays off. Most of the cast lived closer to the theatre, so I appreciated having Barb to hang out with and she knew the area like the back of her hand. On Sundays, Barb and I occasionally went to church together and then out to brunch. As she drove me around the county, picking different areas to visit, she explained the history and culture of the Amish or the Black Bumpers or whomever was living in that area. I was taking it all in because, in my mind, this was my one shot to experience Amish country. In a few short months, I'd be back to city life.

One afternoon she took me back to her home in Strasburg, near the theatre, and proceeded to show me her family pictures. *Wow!* What a huge extended family. She had 20 cousins! She told me the fascinating story from Grandpa Nissley, who was her great-grandfather on her father's side, to the present generation. One family picture included the entire extended family, and she went through all the family members, pointing out and naming each person, while giving me a brief history.

While she was going through the cousins, she stopped at one in particular and said, "That's my cousin Arlin Benner. Now he's a really neat Christian. He went through a tragic time in his life, a divorce in his early 20s, and came to know the Lord through that experience, now he's like a modern day Paul. He teaches Bible studies for men up on the hill where he lives. He said he's never going to remarry; he's going to remain celibate the rest of his life."

"Oh really," I thought to myself, "Celibate from the age of 20-something until forever? Sure would like to see that. Can't say I know of anyone else who would make that proclamation." Then she moved on to the next person in the photograph.

As Barb continued pointing out family members and describing their lives, my mind kept wandering back to Arlin Benner, the 'celibate forever' guy. Fascinating: a modern day Paul, living and breathing right here in Landisville. Just out of curiosity, I wanted to meet him. I interrupted Barb, mid-sentence, and asked her if we could go to one of those Bible studies he taught "on the hill."

"No, they're only for men," she said.

"Interesting," I said out loud. *Chauvinists*, I thought to myself.

Saturday, May 13, 1995

What is the pursuit of happiness? Lord God, so many times I wonder what I am doing at 36, single, and living in what seems to be a temporary situation. Am I just drifting through life because I don't want to commit? I need You to show me. One by one, the days go by in my life and I see that nothing seems to amount to anything. Perhaps I have pursued happiness in the wrong areas and so I keep searching. Maybe I'm not totally surrendered. Is much of my unhappiness caused by self-centeredness? Then I ask You to forgive me, Lord. Teach me to be unselfish. It's really difficult, Father. The Scripture that tells me to "deny myself and take up my cross" is hard. I feel in constant denial of my dreams and desires. It's so hard to have them anymore. Do You want me to? Perhaps not. Many people suffer. I would love a man to lead me, to seek me out for marriage, for us to grow together. But where is that one man? I grow faint and discouraged and very sad and lonely about this.

Sunday, May 14, 1995

Sons are a heritage from the Lord, children a reward from him. Like arrows in the hands of a warrior are sons born in one's youth. Blessed is the man whose quiver is full of them. They will not be put to shame when they contend with their enemies in the gate. (Psalm 127:3–5)

Father, I am not young anymore. Have I lost my heritage of the sons I thought You told me about four years ago? Where are they? Where is my husband? *Blessed is the man whose quiver is full...* I have no quiver, Lord.

Psalm 126:6 reads: "He who goes out weeping, carrying seed to sow, will return with songs of joy, carrying sheaves with him." Lord did I come out of New York City weeping to this place in Lancaster to return married, carrying sheaves with me and songs of joy?! A handsome, very wealthy man, who's relatively older than me, debonair, classy, and charming—and a godly man— is all that too good, Lord? Isn't that every woman's dream? But why would I have a right to have a man like this? Psalm 127:1 reads: "Unless the Lord builds the house, its builders labor in vain. Unless the Lord watches over the city, the watchmen stand guard in vain." Jeremiah 32:27: "I am the Lord, the God of all mankind. Is anything too hard for me?"

Monday, May 15, 1995

Lord, enlarge my tent and give me more faith. I ask for the faith today to believe and receive Your goodness and mercy. I proclaim that I am dead to doubt, fear, and unbelief, but alive to God in Jesus Christ. Father, do you want me to go home—back to Texas, marry there and raise my children around my family? Then I would also have freedom to travel the world and minister. But Lord, I need to know. Who would You bring into my life and how would this happen? I am open to You bringing my husband here to Landisville, Pennsylvania, in Lancaster County. If You want, I could settle here. But please, Lord, make it clear.

The show was going well. Audiences were pouring in by the droves, and, thankfully, they were satisfied by what they had come to see. The most fun for me was the question and answer period after the show each night where the whole cast sat on the edge of the stage and answered questions about the show, usually from five-year-old kids. They invariably wanted to know something about the camel or how long it took to build the ark. The children were in complete awe of the massive structure that was the ark; it really brought this amazing Bible story to life for them. It was so incredible to be a part of the launch production. We all felt part of something really special and knew that this premier was raising Christian theatre to a new level of credibility; it was truly an honor to be part of it.

Now that the show was up and running, a smooth routine had begun to flow into my life. A show in the morning, a dance or voice class in the afternoon, a show at night, a quick dinner, a nice long bubble bath and then off to bed.

As I sat in my candlelit bubbly haven, my mind sometimes mused about this Arlin Benner person. I couldn't help but be intrigued by his character.

Barb had shared a bit about his background. He was a second-generation dairy farmer, hard working and admired by his siblings and others in the Mennonite community. He clearly was a man of God with a good reputation, even with family members. Occasionally, I would think about what it would be like to meet him, to casually run into him at Weis or Turkey Hill. As quickly as those thoughts would dance around my head, I'd chase them away.

I was too busy with my work schedule to even think about entertaining the idea of spending time with a local dairy farmer. After all, I was waiting for my husband, who I was sure was an older man of wealth, distinguished and well-established. I didn't have time for a trivial flirtation, even with a modern day Paul!

Wednesday, May 17, 1995

This is my resting place forever and ever; here I will sit enthroned, for I have desired it. I will bless her with abundant provisions; her poor will I satisfy with food. I will clothe her priests with salvation, and her saints will ever sing for joy. Here I will make a horn grow for David and set up a lamp for my anointed one. I will clothe his enemies with shame, but the crown on his head will be resplendent. (Psalm 132:14–18)

Oh Father, my heart seems to have grown cold with the pain of life and disappointment. I do not feel the urgency to share You or the sense that I'm hurting others who are dying without You. Am I growing cold and bitter? Lord, it has been such a long wait for a husband to come. What I really desire, Lord, is romance! Father, please speak to me. How do I grab more tightly to You in this time? I grow faint of trying to find You. Can You be found more easily? I remember Isaiah 58. Father, forgive me for the pointing finger and malicious talk. Jesus, change my heart and put Your coal to my lips. Let me be silent for three days. Forgive me for not spending myself for the lost and the oppressed. Forgive me, Lord Jesus Christ, for being a stubborn horse, for pulling away from Your lead rope. You spoke and said that my field would be bountiful and my boundaries wide— but I must be led by You. I have rebelled against You and Your commands to love You with all my heart, mind, and soul—and my neighbor as myself. I have loved me and my desires first and foremost.

Two weeks after the show opened, I met a young man named Edward, through Marsha, a friend who worked at the theatre. Edward was hurting emotionally and needed someone to help him. Six weeks after he had married his girlfriend of five years, she divorced him and ran off with a biker. Edward, of course, was devastated and confused, and Marsha thought I might be able to share the Lord with him. I told Marsha Edward needed a man to minister to him, not me. The problem was none of the guys at the theatre felt qualified, and I didn't know any other men in town I could turn to for this sort of thing.

I knew from my quiet time with the Lord that He was calling me to take my mind off of me and to concentrate on "my neighbor." I felt like God was calling me to help this Edward, but I also knew it was a bad idea for a woman to counsel a man on issues of the heart, especially a vulnerable man – and my being a single woman? Not a good idea. So, I called Yvonne to see if she had any ideas about a mature Christian man who could counsel Edward. One of her three sons had attended Bible school and I felt sure she would direct me to him., but she didn't. Instead, she said, "Oh, my nephew Arlin is such a neat Christian man. He leads two or three men's Bible studies weekly, and I'm sure he'd be perfect for your friend."

Arlin Benner, there was that name again! Yvonne was certain he was the man who could help Edward. She gave me his home, farm, and truck phone numbers. Okay, so this 'modern day Paul' teaches two or three men's Bible studies a week. Who is this guy, a saint? He probably has major women issues, I told myself. Forgive me Lord that was just plain mean.

I kept looking at Arlin's phone numbers. I tried to remind myself that this connection was for Edward. "I'm making this call for Edward!" But, I think I knew, even then, that this connection would mean something to me, personally. Every time I reached for the phone to call Arlin, I had a funny feeling in my stomach. I felt like dialing his number was like stepping onto a train about to take a journey to some unknown place. But, I didn't want to go to some unknown place. I wanted to finish my time here and go back to New York City. "Oh dear God, he'd better not be cute! I really don't think I can meet him. Lord, are You up to something? Please, no. I'm going back to New York City!"

Sunday, May 21, 1995

Lord, as I read Psalm 139 and see that You know me from the inside out, I ask You…what is the thing that holds me back? What is it that keeps me from being outside in the habitat that You created for me? I see the bee in my house and how it's not there because it wants to be; it wants to be let out. It goes to the window, but can't get out. I see, Lord, how You answered my prayers this week and I thank You. Maybe I haven't come to You with faith believing You would bless me and set me free. But perhaps I have not really surrendered to You either. What is true surrender, and how do I give in to You? I have asked You to use me, but perhaps I haven't asked You to take me.

"Deborah, surrender your will for your life to Me. You are still pulling away from my lead rope. All these years and you still do not trust Me. I have contended with you and waited all these years. Will you surrender your whole self to Me, including your womanhood, your right to be married and be in love, your right to have what you want, your career, a husband, travel, clothes, thinness, beauty, voice, talent, independence, horses, things, friends, family, and homes? Will you lay it all down and come to Me with empty hands and say, 'Here I am, Lord. Use me'? I am waiting for full surrender. I cannot use a vessel that wants to serve Me—but not love Me or allow Me to love her. You do give Me your body, but you have not given Me your will. Surrender your will to me. That's what I am asking. Surrender your will to Me."

But how, Lord? How do I surrender my will? Show me how. I do not know how to give up that stronghold between us.

"This one, Deborah, I will not deliver you from; you must choose to give Me this."

But, Lord, I need help because I don't even know how I am holding on. Where? And how do I know if I have really given it up?

"Cease from striving and make a choice."

But will it really change?

"Is your choice to gain what you want or to love Me?"

It's to get what I want...

"There you have it. Read about who I am and see if there should be any reason not to trust Me with the results." (Isaiah 47:4, 48:2, 51:15, and 54:5)

All spiritual dilemmas aside, I needed a blender. I mean I was totally preoccupied with finding a blender. I was into making protein shakes to stay healthy and in shape for the physically demanding schedule of the shows. Mixing ingredients by hand was getting old. I needed a blender. So, I called Yvonne and asked her where I could buy one. I had no idea where any stores were. Since I had come to Lancaster, I hadn't really ventured out on my own at all. Basically, my routine was to go to the theatre and return home.

She sent me to a K-mart two small towns away. Living in Landisville meant I had to drive through Mount Joy (all of about two traffic lights) and onto Elizabethtown. She didn't name these little towns, she just told me to stay on Route 230 or Main Street, and I would eventually see the K-mart.

As I hit the first red light in Mount Joy, I turned to my left and there was this big black stretch limousine pulling out from the opposite side of the road. It made a left-hand turn and passed in front of the Dollar General store, right in front of me. "Hmm... God, You must want to show me that You can bring my husband here. He's probably someone famous visiting his mother or some close relative who moved to this area."

As the limo, possibly carrying my future husband, drove out of sight, I continued to drive through town. I looked at the stores on both sides of Main Street; Dollar General was the only store name even remotely recognizable. "What do people do around here for a living?" I muttered. "What do they do for a life? Oh Lord, if I lived here I would slit my wrists!" A stretch limo sighting and a purchase from K-Mart, all in one day; it was like two worlds colliding. I cruised out of town, a little faster, and headed toward K-mart. I was on a mission for a blender—a blender to make me slender. I laughed aloud at my own silly joke which shook me out of my judgmental thoughts. But I was still determined that the next blender I purchased would be from Macy's on 34th Street, in midtown Manhattan.

Chapter 6

Arlin Benner, in the Flesh

Over a period of three weeks, I left two messages on Arlin's machine explaining the situation about Edward. Arlin did not return either of my phone calls. I called Yvonne and said, "Look, your nephew is obviously freaked out about women or something. Why don't you just call him and make sure he gets hooked up with Edward?"

Yvonne assured me that Arlin was probably just busy and she prodded me to continue trying, but I ignored her for three weeks. I convinced myself, the only reason I wanted to meet him personally was to make sure he didn't believe in some bogus religion, but was a real believer. After all, I was introducing him to Edward for spiritual guidance and the last thing I wanted was for Edward to be more confused by some religious wacko too afraid of women to even return a freakin' phone call!

At the end of those three weeks, I was sitting with a couple of friends on my front porch, I said, "You know, who does this guy think he is? If he's such an 'awesome' man of God, he should've returned my call immediately to help Edward! I mean, what the hey?! You'd think he'd want to help the poor guy out. I'm calling him right now." I quickly dialed his number—before I lost my nerve. This time, he answered.

"Is this Arlin Benner in the flesh or did I reach another recording?" I said half-joking. I could tell by his response he was sorry he ever answered. He fumbled around for reasons why he hadn't returned my phone calls. Sure, the electricity went off in his house and erased all his messages and he had failed to write down my number. *Yeah, sorry, buddy. Not buying it.* Finally, he asked me about Edward.

As I was telling him Edward's story, he waited for a pause in our conversation (kind of a long wait) and then said, "I want to hear about you and how you came to know the Lord."

"Uhhh…" I said. Beyond that, I was speechless. I was not prepared for that! All I wanted to do was to share what was necessary about Edward and his situation; I did not want to talk about me, much less my personal testimony. But here I was, with Arlin Benner on the other end of the line, and he wanted to know about me. In the silence, that seemed eternal, I had to ask myself, "Why don't I just relax, let go and answer the man's question?"

For the life of me, I couldn't come up with a legitimate reason why I shouldn't! So, I quickly regained composure and launched into the brief (okay, 45- minute) version of my personal life. After a long pause, he said, "Well, listen. They're having a revival meeting tonight down at The Camp Woods in the large open-air tabernacle where you live. My mom talked me into being a counselor for those who come up for prayer at the end of the meeting. Are you busy tonight? We could meet after." My turn for a long pause, I mentally ran through my schedule. I had an afternoon show. I could shower after and meet him at the revival, but not until 8:30 p.m. I told him, and, to my surprise, he said that would work fine.

"But, since we've never met, how will we find each other?" I asked. Barb had shown me her family picture way back in May. But, everyone's face was about the size of a tiny button, I had no idea what he looked like. He was one of about 50 or 60 people. It reminded me of one of those high school graduation class pictures where everyone is lined up in rows and it looks like they're about a mile away. The Amish and Mennonites have *lots* of kids, but, so do the Italians, we just don't take class pictures together.

"Don't worry. I'll find you," he replied. Okay, I was intrigued. I like a man who takes charge and doesn't worry about the details, like what I look like! "Oh Lord! Please let him be ugly, please don't let me be attracted to him in any way. I was tortured by my inner conflict; a powerful man of God, sure of himself in every way, and interested in meeting me – but, a dairy farmer? I'm not going to date a guy who milks cows for a living and risk falling in love, marrying him and then be stuck living on some hill in Landisville, Pennsylvania for the rest of my life. I simply am not!"

I spent more time than I should have getting ready that night and went off to the tent meeting. It was packed. I sat outside the open-air tabernacle on a picnic table with Yvonne and her husband, Wayne; her sister-in-law, Eileen; and Lamar and Holly, two of her other relatives. My back was to the tabernacle, but I noticed a guy who kept looking over at me. *That must be him. Yuck, I thought* and *Great! He's a geeky-looking typical Christian guy. I'll check him out, make sure he's not really a Hare Krishna or something weird, and then give him over to Edward.* Now, calling him a"geeky-looking typical Christian guy" was totally from my perspective; seeing people, situations, and so forth from our own perspectives can sometimes be pretty narrow-minded. I had experienced though, in the realm of dating, that some of the Christian guys I had met were a little geeky, while all the cool guys with looks to-die-for and "their lives together" weren't Christians.

The meeting ended, and I could feel someone approaching. I put on my all-business smile, expecting to see the geeky guy. But when I turned, the geeky guy was nowhere in sight. Instead, there stood Arlin with his million-dollar smile! He was *gorgeous!* I was a mess. I've heard the description of knees buckling, but I actually had to lean against the picnic table to keep my balance.

Oh, no, not him, Lord! Come on. Give me a break here, would ya?!

I heard myself talking to him, but it was as if I was hearing my voice through a tunnel. I had no idea what I was saying; I just couldn't stop staring at his teeth. Those beautiful white teeth; that smile! When I did steal a look at his eyes, they twinkled. He smiled and I blushed. I haven't blushed since I was in third grade. I was getting absolutely pathetic, but I couldn't help myself. I was captive to my own heart which was, presently, melting. Suddenly, I remembered what the Holy Spirit had spoken to me nine months earlier, while walking down Madison Avenue on my way to work that one evening. "I'm bringing your husband."

"Now I'm not sure I remember your name. It's Deb, right?" he asked as he extended his hand to shake mine.

"No, it is Debo*rah*," I said, forcing some sort of propriety, extending my hand to shake his.

He raised an eyebrow with a glint in his eye, and we shook hands. I had a moment to take inventory. "Oh, no, Lord. This can't be him! Yes, he's gorgeous, but God, he's a dairy farmer, in Podunk, PA! But, okay. I do like his hands—nice, strong, smooth, pretty. I hate ugly hands. And he looks pretty darn fine in jeans, and he has good taste – I like his shirt—and he's got great hair."

How's that for a "godly" response?

He had a friend with him, Willy, who seemed like a nice guy, but wouldn't leave Arlin's side. Barb had previously explained Arlin never went anywhere without one or two guy friends with him. Apparently, he was the "catch" of the county – a single guy in his 30s, a successful farmer, just a perfect husband. Since, in his mind, he wasn't going to remarry, he *always* brought one of his "bodyguards" along to ward off any wanting women.

Before meeting Arlin, my response was, *"Oh Romeo, give me a break!"* But,now, standing here before him, my thought was. *"Oh, Lord, give me a break!"* Suddenly, Arlin became all business and focused on the task at hand – Edward. At that point, I was thinking, "Edward, who?" However, I quickly matched his tone and we set up a meeting for the following Wednesday. The plan was to have Edward and Arlin over to meet for coffee on my front porch, right after my evening performance. Then he—rather abruptly—said his goodbyes and he and Willy left. Our first meeting lasted about 12 minutes.

I was devastated. Apparently our face-to-face meeting was not doing to his knees what it was obviously doing to mine!

When I got home, I called my folks in Texas and cried on the phone saying, "Mom, I think I just met my husband! But he doesn't know I exist and worse than that, he's a dairy farmer! "

She just laughed and said, "Now, of course he knows you exist. You just blew him away. He's never met such a beautiful woman who's so strong and on fire for the Lord. He didn't know what to do with you, just wait, you'll see, he'll be calling you.... Now what was that again about him being a farmer?" I rolled my eyes as my stomach turned. I had to get off the phone. I assured mom I'd be okay, told her I loved her and I'd call tomorrow. I hung up, still dazed.

I flung myself on my bed and stared at the ceiling. I really felt certain God was moving my heart toward this man. But why would He do this if Arlin wasn't feeling the same about me? Then I tried to encourage myself. Maybe I was reading him wrong, there could still be hope. Maybe God will move in his heart, too, then I got scared. Well, what if he did fall for me, what would that mean? Okay, we'd date, fall in love, I'd move here, permanently, we'd get married… Oh, no! I'd be married to a dairy farmer! I started to cry all over again.

Now, I had nothing against dairy farmers, but the idea of marrying one had never entered my mind. Trust me. In all the years and with all the scenarios I had imagined, I never envisioned the Lord reserving a dairy farmer just for me. And I could only guess what it would be like to move from New York City to the farm. Correction: I couldn't guess. I had *no idea!*

But I liked this guy. There was definitely something about him that was absolutely fresh and new and completely different from any other man I had dated, or had even been attracted to. It seemed as if Wednesday would never come. I could not wait to see Arlin again. I thought about him constantly. Every performance I had, I felt as if I was sleepwalking through it. My body was performing all the routines, I was saying my lines, but my mind was in another hemisphere.

Finally, Wednesday came, and when Arlin stepped up onto my front porch, my heart began to race. I was bringing out coffee to Edward and Marsha who had just arrived. Arlin sat down and I was sure they could all guess what I was thinking as I stole a look at his chest when he reached for his cup of coffee. Luckily, no one seemed to notice anything strange; even though I stopped talking mid-sentence, preoccupied by how his hands gripped the cup I had given him. My secret was safe, for now.

I began to relax and put my attention on Edward and the real reason for our gathering. Edward shared his story with Arlin. Arlin sympathized with Edward's situation and shared some personal insight from his own experiences. Arlin was beautifully transparent and unashamed as he talked about the struggle he had also in those early months after divorce. I began to see this other side of him; the person leading all the Bible studies and having the reputation of being a modern day Paul. Not only was I attracted to this man, I was drawn to his soul.

The night was going well. Everyone felt safe sharing and we continued chatting for a few hours, enjoying our coffee and getting more acquainted. Arlin invited us to come to the Bible study he taught on Thursday evenings at Willy's house, since women were allowed to attend that one, hallelujah! Edward already had plans, but Marsha and I said yes.

After they all had left, I couldn't sleep. Normally I was exhausted after a long day of performances, but tonight, I was invigorated. I kept replaying the evening and the conversation in my head. I allowed my mind to linger a little longer on the memory of Arlin's words, his facial expression, his quick and easy smile... I decided I'd better turn to the Lord before my mind got me into any real trouble. I began to look back over my journal and found a word the Lord had spoken to me only a few weeks before.

Thursday, July 26, 1995

"Deborah, even now you are seeing how I do tax the ends of the earth to bring about My purposes for your life. You may rest and trust in this that I do in your life. You are seeing only the beginning of what I have for your life to move and work through you and in you for My kingdom. Yes, I know the time yesterday in Mount Joy was to show you that I can bring him to you. I have the day and the hour and the time set. I know you are growing weary in the waiting and are impatient and excited for this new season to dawn in your life. It is coming and you must wait for it. He will love you with an everlasting love because it will be My love through him to you. You will experience Me in the way you have longed for through this man. As you have poured out your love to others, my love through you, now I will pour

out to you for this man. You are not crazy or having vain imaginations. Ponder My great work in your heart and continue to ponder this work until I have completed it. It will heal your heart and you will no longer feel the pain of women who have used their positions or social status to put you under. Neither will you use your newfound position to hurt others."

The next night when I got home, I did something totally uncharacteristic; I initiated a meeting with a man! I called Arlin and left a message, inviting him for coffee Friday evening at my place—of course, I extended the invitation to his bodyguard/friend. Arlin left a message later saying he had a previous commitment but that he would take a rain check for Saturday after he finished counseling at The Camp Woods. I then left another message confirming Saturday. What a game of telephone tag for such a simple meeting!

When I came home from the theatre that Saturday, it was about 10:30 p.m., and Arlin was not yet at my house. I walked over to the tabernacle and found him and his youngest brother, Loren, chatting. They followed me back to my place with another friend of theirs, Roger. My porch was quite the meeting place. I did have absolutely the cutest porch ever, perfect for entertaining.

We had a great time again chatting and getting to know one another, although this time, it was light conversation. No one was spilling family secrets or anything, but I still felt nervous. He still hadn't given me any indication that he might be remotely interested. I thought he was just being friendly, getting to know someone new. I didn't learn anything personal about him, or any of them for that matter, we just visited.

At the end of the evening, Arlin invited me to come to his church the following day, Sunday, and I agreed. I was anxious, and I didn't sleep most of the night. A million thoughts raced through my head. I had been journaling like mad ever since meeting him. But tonight, I didn't. I just lay in bed, staring up at my ceiling, begging God to show me if this feeling I had about Arlin was real.

On the way to his church, I was shaking in my boots, or in my case, pricey high heels. Who was this guy? How was he able to make me feel this way? What was I getting myself into? I arrived just as the service was beginning, so we had no time to visit. He looked so handsome all dressed up in his classy suit! The worship was incredible. I remember standing and just praising God. I had never felt happier in my entire life. Of course, I did feel a little awkward. What if he thought I was strange or something? After all, nobody else in the church was standing, raising their hands, praising God. I made up my mind to just focus on God and put those thoughts out of my head.

He asked if I had plans after the service. "Well, yes, I am supposed to meet some friends at my place and from there we're all going to brunch together at the Railroad House."

"Oh," he said.

"Well, would you like to join us? You can come, too," I added quickly. He agreed. Was I nuts? Had I really just invited him to go along with us? I was scared—no, petrified! Was I making a new friend, getting a new buddy, or speaking to my future husband?

I told him he would have to drive back to my house, but I needed to follow him because I didn't know my way back. I had gotten lost getting there and was clueless as to the return trip home. First of all, I had his infamous farmer's directions, which comprised the eighth wonder of the world. Then there were the endless farms, pastures, chicken houses, and churches I passed to finally arrive at his church. There were no "red shoes" to click together three times. Plenty of mooing cows, but no Toto to take me home.

Chapter 7

Confirmation, Please

When we arrived at my cottage, no one was there. I don't know who was more freaked out: he or I. It was our first time alone together. We went inside, and I ran upstairs to change while he waited downstairs in the kitchen. In the meantime, my mom called. What timing that woman has! I went downstairs to use the kitchen phone and told him it was my mother. He shouted from the background, "Hi, Mom!" Was that a prophetic statement or just being cute? Either way, it made my heart race. I was so close to blurting out my feelings for him, I scared myself.

Thank GOD, I didn't...

After I hung up, Arlin said something that really aggravated me: "I don't ever want to be married. Why would one pathetic person want to live with another pathetic person?" First of all, did I miss something? Were we talking about marriage? No! Who the heck was saying anything aloud about marriage and where did that statement come from?

"Well, *you* may be pathetic, but *I'm* not," I fired back. I had plenty more of those on hand, I'm Italian. He'd better get used to the fact that I say what I think; friends, buddies or lifelong partners, I call it like I see it. "I know one thing," I continued. "The Bible says that the man who finds a good wife is blessed. And *I'm* good-wife material, *not* a pathetic person." After the words escaped my lips, I got nervous. Had I gone too far? Did I just blow it? My mind shifted again! "Well, who cares?" I thought. I didn't wait this long to become someone's pathetic... anything!

Boy, just who did he think he was? Now I was really annoyed... and downright confused. If God had truly spoken to my heart about this man, God sure had his work cut out for Him. This guy was so paranoid about women and marriage you would need a steamroller to set his mind straight. I felt ready to kick him off my porch.

Thank God that Marsha, Brenda, and Edward arrived, and the new faces softened the mood, and everyone was pleasantly surprised to see Arlin. I explained how I had invited him to join us for brunch. Arlin offered to drive all three women in his car, leaving Edward to follow in his truck. Sounded like a stacked deck to me! I could feel the wave of anger rising to the top of my head. However, all anyone else could see was my sweet southern smile, which I pasted on as I climbed in the *backseat* of Arlin's car. I kept catching his gaze in the rearview mirror. Was he smiling? I could only see his eyes, but I could feel him smiling. He was enjoying this! I could feel the steam starting to blow out my ears, but I just looked at him in the mirror and gave him a huge smile, right back! Two can play your toothy-grin game, buddy. You just met your match.

As we entered the restaurant, I caught a glimpse of Arlin's shoes. *Oh, good, dorky shoes… Clearly, he's not my husband.* How could he have on a perfectly gorgeous European suit and dorky shoes? All right, all right, I know, I was looking for stuff, but, they were dorky shoes and I didn't check my sense of style at the door. Call me superficial, but I was looking for anything that would make him less attractive to me; the shoes were working.

The five of us sat around the table. Arlin sat next to me and across from Marsha. During the entire brunch, he directed much of his conversation to her. He rarely even glanced in my direction. I was upset with myself by how much this affected me. I was disappointed and started to feel extremely ridiculous. He must be interested in her. That's probably better because she is from here and probably has had a thing for him her whole life. They'll have more in common, and they'll be able to see each other. Because in a couple of months, I'm out of here and back in New York City! Maybe that was my sole purpose in coming to Pennsylvania, to bring Arlin together with Marsha! Thank you, God, for using me in this noble way…*Oh, who did I think I was kidding?* I was so upset it felt like my guts were coming out, but I managed to contain myself, keeping cool and acting like everything was just great.

As we finished brunch, he paid for everyone, and the bill was over $100. I couldn't believe it, and I felt bad because these weren't even his friends. Well, that was certainly not necessary, but mighty gentlemanly; he's now one for two. The day was young; maybe he could totally redeem himself by sundown.

We all climbed back in the car; I called front seat, that time by eyeballing my friends. There was that smile of his. Did he know he was getting to me? As we drove along, the scenery was absolutely beautiful. The corn in the fields on either side of the winding country road was in full bloom—as in about ten feet tall! He drove us by some of his cornfields, and I told him I wanted to pick some to have as a memory before I left for home in New York City, in just a few short months. I really just wanted more time with him. He stopped and picked one ear of corn for me, but told us it was not for eating. All the corn he planted was feed for the cows. He planted a field of sweet corn every year for his family, but the rest was cow feed for the coming year.

Then he proceeded to take us to see his place. At first I could tell he was a little hesitant, but then he drove up the quarter-mile steep driveway to his house. I was expecting a somewhat mid-size beautiful house. After seeing all the large farm homes in the county, I just assumed that his would be the same.

I didn't know his parents remained in the original farmhouse and he had moved off the property. Arlin's land was part of the original farm, which had been deeded off and was about a mile down the road, around the corner from where he grew up. Rounding the last bend, we pulled up to a single-wide mobile home on the top of a hill. No flowers, no pots with flowers in them, a few bushes, no color, just a brown mobile home on a hill; not much curb appeal. Well, that sealed the coffin shut.

Arlin was clearly not my husband. I knew for sure God was bringing me a man of means; this was not him. Living just off Fifth Avenue in New York to a *single-wide* trailer in Cowville, Pennsylvania? I don't think so.

I figured Arlin, being in his 30s and a business owner, would have built a nice house—or just a house—by now. Then I could have just moved right in and had everything all ready. God, I'm not 20 just starting out my life; I'm 37… Thirty-seven! I pictured Him sitting on His throne having a laugh at me, in a loving father's way, but laughing, nonetheless. If God were Italian, the scene would be Him in a rocker, on the veranda, smoking His cigar. That thought gave me a giggle and some comfort.

"Oh Lord, I could *never* live here! You know what, God? It's *much* better he likes Marsha because I just couldn't live in this place. I mean, come on! It's one thing to leave New York and move to a dairy farm, but a trailer? Just who do You think I am? I mean, You made me, God! Surely, You don't have this in mind for me…do You?" I asked this question sheepishly. Too many times I had experienced the unexpected. But this was beyond all un-expectations.

I may have lived on a $10-a-day budget, but I lived in a beautiful rent-controlled apartment and I simply adored my little 85-year-old Jewish landlord. He had been born and raised in this townhouse before he converted it into apartments. I was so blessed to rent from him. One time he even *lowered* my rent because I could not afford the increase! Tell me that's not a miracle. What landlord in New York City *lowers* the rent? *None!*

The land Arlin lived on, however, was magnificent: five acres with a stream running through the front of the property, winding around the back, surrounded by nearly 100-foot trees everywhere. So beautiful - but the trailer? Yikes! I'm sure Marsha would do a great job giving it a woman's touch, I mused.

Coming down his driveway, he told us about how he was preparing to go into the trucking business with his two older brothers, and he too would be moving away soon, to be closer to the business. I immediately had a check in my spirit about this business venture, which seemed odd, because I barely knew the man. I discerned—rather, the Spirit of God in me discerned—that this was the wrong move.

He drove us through a few covered bridges on the way home. It was enchanting, and reminded me of *The Bridges of Madison County*, a love story that began on a covered bridge. Finally, he dropped us off at my place. I was surprised by how much I wanted to just touch him. It was so ridiculous, but I really needed to have some sort of physical contact. So I said, "Well, we all have to hug him good-bye and thank him for taking us out and buying our brunch." He said, "That's okay, no one has to hug me."

"No," I said, "We don't *have* to hug you, but we want to, since you were so generous today, driving us around, buying brunch." We all gave him a hug despite his protests. When my turn came, I didn't want to let go. I was thinking of every excuse in the world to get him to stay and visit with us, but nothing came to mind. Okay, Einstein, what happened to the creative flow? Gone.

At brunch, he reminded us about the Bible study he taught on Thursdays at Willy's house. He emphasized that he really wanted us to come, and we confirmed we would be there.

I could hardly wait for Thursday to come…

Chapter 8

Let It Be Him

Sunday, August 6, 1995

Lord, what an incredible journey it has been these last few days. Arlin Benner came into my life one week ago Sunday and it has changed me. I am moved by his passion for You and his love for You. I am also very attracted to him physically. But, Lord, I don't want to disturb Your work in his life or mine. I do not want to be his stumbling block, or he mine. I have thoughts and desires for him already! Today, I couldn't eat as he shared his heart about You and his tears over Your work in his life. I love his heart. In the natural, I'm not excited that he's a farmer and has no formal education, has not traveled the world, and doesn't speak another language. He took us today to see covered bridges like in the novel The Bridges of Madison County. Oh Father! So many mixed emotions I'm feeling. Help me to sort out truth—Your truth. Help me not to stir up love until its time. My stomach was in knots today at the brunch table. I loved when he was trying to explain things and would smile and look for just the right words. I'm disturbed in my spirit, or perhaps my flesh, because he doesn't fit my picture or thoughts or preconceived ideas of what I believe You have set aside for me. I've always known You to give me diamonds in the rough. He is not a sophisticated man. But...he is humble of heart, simple, with a passion for You. Lord, help me to rightly discern this situation. Take away any hint of a spark for this man if it is not Your will! You can help me focus and keep on track. Help me not to get "wigged out"... You are doing such marvelous work in my life, and I don't want that to end.

I need You to stick close to me. What is this one about? I have been so deceived in the past. Only You could know and understand the heart and plans of man. Only You could bring about Your will and purposes for all our lives. Let Your will be done, Father. Let Your will be done. And give me the grace and strength to accept Your will. Father, of course, I would like him to call me. Will he? As he seeks You, speak to him about me. What is he thinking? Only You know. Only You— and I'm glad it's You who knows the truth. I love You, Father, and I praise You for this beautiful season in my life.

Tuesday, August 8, 1995

Father, when I grasp for a moment Your sacrifice on the cross for me, it almost makes me physically ill. It hurts to receive how much You love me. I do need to stay focused on the work You are doing in my heart. It does motivate me to do anything Your will desires. It gives me strength to say "Yes" to someone like Arlin knowing You have our destiny in Your hands. One thing You have taught me is to trust Your leading and Your choices for me. Father, I do love You and I do desire that You would help me to receive Your goodness. It's really tough for me. Forgive me for all the wrong choices I have made. Father, I am trying so hard to keep my thoughts only on You. I confess that every time the phone rang today, I hoped it was Arlin. But how silly. I have to keep my thoughts captive to my work, Your work in me. Lord, I give You Arlin. I hold my hands open. As I conversed with Carol today at the dance studio, we talked about a man being after Your own heart and how appealing that is—and exciting. I thank You, Lord, for Arlin's desire for You and the way he has run after You. Continue to call him and give him a thirst and hunger for You. That's the most attractive thing about him. I must give You my obsessive thoughts about him.

Help me, Father. I can tell You and pour out my heart to You because I know now in my heart You desire to answer me and take my case for me. Father, if Your plan is to put Arlin and me together, please speak to his heart and give him the strength to overcome any doubts he might have. I know he might feel uncertain because we come from two different backgrounds. Lord, I don't want to settle either if You have something else for me. I'm willing to begin a relationship with him and return to New York City and carry on long distance. I'm willing to let time and distance pass between us and for me to go on with what You have for my life. Father, I pour out my heart to You. I desire to hear from him and can hardly wait until Thursday. I wish he would come for dinner tomorrow night or that there would be a message on my answering machine this evening when I return home. Father, don't be angry with me that I still desire a man. I don't want my affections for a man to compete with You. I'm not sure how to balance these desires, except that I am overwhelmingly receiving Your goodness now and am learning to draw near to You in a new way, a more intimate way. "Daughter, you may enter my courts with thanksgiving and praise, for I delight in you." Father, will You speak to him about me today as he's driving among the fields?

The next day, Monday, my day off other than Sundays, I sent Arlin a thank-you note for the brunch. Since I met Arlin, my routine had changed. As soon as I would get home, I'd hurry in the house to check and see if he had called. When I saw the light blinking, I prayed, "Let it be him." For two days, no call from Arlin.

Then finally, Wednesday, the light was blinking! I quickly pressed the button, listened, then smiled. It was his voice! He said he received my thank you note, thanked me for it and said he wanted to remind me about the Bible study the next day. Like I could forget… I returned his call that night. He was home, small miracle, and we chatted.

As our conversation became more comfortable, I carefully questioned him about his new business venture with his brothers. I couldn't tell him it was wrong. After all, who was I? I had only just met him ten days earlier. But, the Holy Spirit in me knew this move wasn't right. I asked him what the Bible had to say about partnerships. He said, "I don't know. I never really thought about it. Why don't you tell me?"

"No," I said. "You'll have to search the Scriptures for yourself or else it won't be your own revelation—it will only be what I tell you it says." He kept asking me to just tell him, so I did. I explained how from what I could gather when searching the Word to gain guidance about business, God continues to make it clear in His design. He does not have all chiefs and no Indians in His business. You can't have two heads, or they will generally always be fighting. God gave each man his own business or made him an employee of another's. Just look at our forefathers such as Abraham, Isaac, Jacob, or David and all the kings. Or, look at Joseph, from the dungeon to Pharaoh's number-one guy. Most successful businessmen surround themselves with brilliant managers and employees. Arlin was silent.

I believed purchasing the trucking business would show a lack of wisdom, but I knew Arlin would have to make that decision for himself. I asked him if I could pray for him. Arlin said yes, so I did. Afterward, he said he had never heard anyone pray like that before in his life. Boy, the Lord was really making me look good! Before he hung up, he asked me if I would bring my guitar to the Bible study and lead praise and worship. That made me a little nervous, but I agreed.

Every minute seemed like a day as I waited for Thursday night to arrive and I'd get to see Arlin again. By this time, I had told my closest friends in New York and my family in Texas about him. I shared with them that I believed this was the man God had created for me and me for him. Only when was God going to tell him?

I joined Marsha and another friend, Peggy, and we met Arlin and a couple of his friends in a parking lot near the theatre. I hadn't said a word to Marsha about how I felt about Arlin or what God was showing me. What if she was interested in him? She hadn't mentioned it, but one never knows, and I would never compete for a man. Besides, I didn't have to. If he was mine and the one God had for me, then he was mine; nothing could change that.

When we got to Willy's, I couldn't believe how beautiful his place was. We drove through cornfields with stalks 12 feet high to a swimming pool in the middle of nowhere with a pavilion where the men had started a barbecue. The moon was full. It was a beautiful, romantic evening.

I played my guitar and led worship for about 25 minutes. Afterward, Arlin taught the study. I could tell he was very nervous. I was hoping it was my presence there, but I still didn't have a read on him. Was he interested or not? He was doing a superb job of keeping me from having any suspicion that he might be considering me.

He had shown us where the outdoor bathroom was and warned us about spiders. When he said that, he made his hand crawl on my back. *Wait a minute! Was he flirting with me?* Yes! Okay, he was pretending to be a spider, but he touched me, voluntarily! Not a big thing for most guys, but for Arlin Benner, I knew it was huge. Yes! That was indeed a playful, flirtatious thing to do. Yippee!

But then, I was scared. I knew if I responded, things would be set into motion. This thing that I had prayed for, for 17 years— marriage, future, the biggest change of my life – could really begin to happen! Was I ready? Could I handle this *udder*, I mean *utter*, and complete transformation in my life? Could I make all the necessary adjustments?

It's so amazing. While I'm waiting for God's plan to come to pass, I feel like it never will. Then, suddenly, out of nowhere it's upon me, new territory, uncharted waters, unsafe ground, but was I prepared?

I giggled appropriately at his spider crawl up my back, I grabbed his hand for a moment, and our eyes locked. We both smiled. Yep, something was happening. No turning back, now.

The Bible study was ending and people were beginning to make their way back to their cars. Again, I was racking my brain trying to think of an excuse to stay; I didn't want to leave him, I had none. *Oh ye woman of such great faith and so few excuses!* Before we left, he invited us to attend his church on Sunday, we all said we would be there.

When I got home that night, I couldn't sleep. I didn't want to bring my girlfriends with me to his church. I was hoping for an opportunity to be alone with him, hoping he would ask me to go to brunch so I could finally get a read on him and, time was running out. The show closed at the end of October, which was just two and a half months away. I needed to know for sure if this was God's man for me—quickly—because, if not, I was going back to the city and would not be returning.

I called my father in Texas, and asked him what he thought I should do about the church situation. Do I take my friends to Arlin's church or do I tell them I prefer if they don't come? Arlin invited all of us at the same time; it wasn't my prerogative to tell them they couldn't come, was it? Dad's answer surprised me. He said that Arlin sounded like the guy he and mother had been praying for all my life. He went on to say that I should tell my friends plainly that I wanted to be alone with Arlin. In particular, I wanted Marsha to stay home! I couldn't believe it. Was that the right thing to do?

I have a very close relationship with my parents, and I've always trusted God to guide me through my father's advice. I knew this was a biblical principle and, if followed, would not fail me. This was a test; it just seemed strange for me to say, "Hi, Marsha. I know Arlin invited us to attend his church on Sunday, but you can't come. I want to be alone with him." That was going to go over like a lead brick!

The next day, Friday, I struggled all morning with calling Marsha. I called my dad several more times to confirm what he had said. He was starting to heat up and getting a little cranky. Did I mention he's Italian? He couldn't understand what my problem was. Finally, I called him at his office and his secretary said, "Your dad's in surgery." (My father's a surgeon.) So, I called the operating room, did I mention, I'm Italian?

They piped my voice in while he was doing surgery. I asked him again what he thought I should do. He said, "I don't know why you are having such a dilemma telling your girlfriend that you don't want her to go with you because you want to be alone with Arlin! Look, you're going riding, right? Take your horse out to pasture for a walk and pray and ask God what to do!"

Well, I was about to go riding, but I didn't have the heart to tell my dad that I was just taking lessons—which meant that I just couldn't say, "Oh and by the way, after my lesson, can I take the horse out for a walk in the pasture so I can talk to God?" I thanked dad, again, he mumbled something and told his nurse to hand him something. Conversation over, I hung up.

I went for my lesson, anyway. When I was through, my trainer came up to me and felt my horse and said, "He's overheated. Why don't you take him for a walk out in the pasture until he cools down? Then you can wash him and put him in his stall." *That God of ours is incredible!* He makes a way where there is no way!

So, I did as she instructed and took my horse out to pasture. As we walked, I took in, again, this breathtakingly beautiful place surrounded by open fields, outlined by neighboring farms. There were rows of corn on one side and grazing cows on the other. In the quiet, I looked up and said, "All right, God, You probably have about 15 minutes to break through to me here and tell me what to do." This was one of those times I needed a burning bush. This was a step of faith that I hadn't graduated to—not yet, anyway.

I felt Him say, "Deborah, you're so afraid. You're afraid to let go. You have become so accustomed to My leading, both through your father and through My one-on-one talks with you. You fear having to be led by a man you know nothing about. But you must know one thing. It's not his leading you will be following, but My leading through him. I'm not letting you go, but now I will be leading you through him. It's still My leading. You can trust Me. You don't have to be afraid. I'm not leaving you."

I didn't even realize what was going on in my own heart. This thing— marriage, God's marriage—was upon me. He had planned this for me since the beginning of time, and I was frightened. I was learning I didn't need to be afraid. God wasn't going anywhere; I knew what I had to do.

That afternoon, I went to the theatre and was determined to tell my friend she couldn't attend Arlin's church on Sunday. I was concerned she would be upset with me. Arlin had become her friend as much as mine. I hadn't confided in her of all I had gone through emotionally since meeting him twelve days earlier, nor had I told her what God had shown me from my first meeting with Arlin. All of these things I had chosen to not share with anyone except my family in Texas and friends in New York. They were far enough removed to use as sounding boards, and none of them knew Arlin, so I could vent or gush, as my moods dictated.

All evening at the theatre I looked for the opportunity to tell Marsha, and it never came. Finally, a fellow actor, who had become a good friend, met me in the break room and said, "Deb, I sense you're really upset about something. God is telling me to tell you that you must do what He tells you to do and not worry about what anybody else thinks or says." He then got up and left the break room, that was the added push I needed.

I walked backstage to find Marsha to tell her that I wanted to go to church alone with Arlin, I found her. I took a silent deep breath, tapped Marsha on the shoulder, and spilled it all out as soon as she turned to me. I knew if I didn't talk fast, I would lose my nerve, but talking fast didn't really soften the blow. Marsha became really upset and began giving me all the reasons she wanted to come along. In the kindest way possible, I stood my ground and said, "Look, I'm sorry. I'm going alone and I don't want you to come. I need to be alone with him." I realized my tone was a little sterner than I had intended. I finally asked her to sit down. We both sat on a bench by the backstage door. I explained that I was interested in him and, since the day I met him, I hadn't had the opportunity to get to know him, one on one.

Marsha didn't look at me, but she nodded. "I knew this was going to happen," she said. I was thinking, "Really? Because until five minutes ago, I didn't know this was going to happen." But she explained, further. "When I saw the way he looked at you at the Bible study, I knew he was interested, I just didn't want to believe it."

My heart skipped a beat! How could Marsha see what I was so desperate to see, but simply couldn't? She got up to leave, but then turned back. A resigned smile crossed her face, "You guys are going to make a cute couple." She walked away— which was a good thing, because I was absolutely speechless.

Chapter 9

Divine Arrangement

Saturday, August 12, 1995

Here I am, Lord, with You, alone at 11 p.m. on a Saturday night. You and I just had a candlelight bath together. I remember the one You and I took when I was dating Paul, and You called me at 3 a.m. in the morning to come take a candlelight bath with You. You spoke to me then about worthiness. Sometimes, Lord, I miss those days. I love what You have done in my life and how good You have been to me. I don't want our journey together and our marriage to ever end. I do feel more than ever now Your bride. And I know a man on this earth is only temporary. He cannot meet this deep need that You do. You are so good to me; I don't know how to explain or contain Your goodness toward me. I pray I can remain ever thankful for Your work in my life!

It is so good what You have done and continue to do. Why do I ever doubt You? I give You Arlin tonight. Though I am attracted to him and would like to get to know him, I know You have my best interests at heart and I do not want to lose focus. I fear that I have lost focus since I met him two weeks ago. I don't want to cut short my journey here or my healing and Your work in my life. What a struggle to maintain that focus. Lord, help me to be only where You want me to be. I love You, Father. I do want You more than a man or temporary fulfillment. Help me to be strong and not weak in this area. Only Your magnificent plan could be for me. I don't want to sell myself—or You—short. I will not talk myself into wanting Arlin. He is, perhaps, not all that wonderful. I want the truth to unfold with this one, Lord, in Your timing. I let go of any of my own manipulation or devices. This one cannot be from You—he is so different from me! We do not have anything in common except You. Everything else is different. It's too vast a difference. That makes me sad. But the truth is, as far as I can see, I do not understand how this would be possible. Only Your hand, Lord. Please reveal this early so I may move on. Help me to keep my heart and my will open to You and Your will for my life.

Sunday morning, I was up about 5am walking the mile-and-a-half drive around The Camp Woods. Lately, I hadn't been able to sleep much, and I had gotten into the habit of walking this path for an hour on a daily basis. On this particular morning, I needed to talk with God in the wee hours with a clear heart, because I was scared.

After my walk, I needed about two hours to pick out what to wear. I wanted to look feminine, but still conservative. I wanted him to notice me, but I didn't want to draw attention to myself – no designer stilettos for me, that Sunday. After all, I was going after a Mennonite! Oh dear, just the thought of it seemed ridiculous! Finally, I picked out a simple skirt that showed my shape—a little—and a feminine blouse.

When I walked into the sanctuary, Arlin came right up to me and, without hesitation, gave me an awesome hug. He pulled back and looked at me. "Sorry, was that okay? I just had to hug you."

"Uh, yes, uh, fine," I stuttered back to him.

How unusual for him! I've never seen him touch a woman, much less give her a hug. Yvonne told me he made a habit of never touching a woman, so no one would get the idea he was even remotely interested, a policy of which I was thankful. Not only did I hate the thought of him hugging other women, I was sure his hugging me actually meant something!

We sat next to each other. I could barely sit still, I was so nervous. The entire time I prayed that he would ask me to brunch afterward. Not very spiritual, I know, but this was big stuff. How was I supposed to pay attention or concentrate on the sermon from the pulpit when God was doing something right here in the pew next to me? Church ended, and as we were walking out Arlin asked, "Are you hungry?"

"Starving!" I said. He barely got the words out before I answered.

"Well, I only have one hour because I have to go back to work today, but do you want to go out and grab a quick bite to eat?" he asked.

"Yes!"

He suggested we go in his truck and then he would take me back to the church later for my car. When we arrived, he had left his wallet in the truck and said he needed to go back and get it. I told him not to; lunch was on me since the week before he had paid for me and all my friends. We sat down to eat and talked and talked and talked! He asked about my life in New York, my work here, what I liked about acting, what I hated about it. I asked him about the farm, what he hated about it, what he liked about it. I laughed when he told me he wasn't really sure what he liked about it.

But then I pressed a little harder, looking for what joy it must bring him. His answer surprised me. He said, "I like that it's mine. I have to make the decisions and decide what happens on the farm, but ultimately I depend completely on milk production which means, I have to put my trust in a bunch of cows." He laughed and then smiled and continued with a more serious tone, "Which means, I really have to have complete trust in our Lord, and listen to his direction in every situation that comes up on the farm... or any place else." He looked at me with intent, and I blushed.

He realized an hour had come and gone and quickly excused himself to use the phone. He left his cell in the truck so he used the phone in the restaurant. He needed to tell one of his hired men to "run out feed for the cows," because he was running late and would be there shortly.

He returned to the table smiling and shaking his head and said, "You're not going to believe this! This never happens. My hired man, who had the day off, forgot his paycheck this morning, and went back to the farm to pick it up. He answered the barn phone when I called and said not to worry about the afternoon chores. He would take care of them so I could stay and enjoy my lunch!"

God had made a way where there was no way for Arlin and me to spend time alone together. We both smiled. I knew he was thinking that exact thing. We were there for three more hours! He did ask me one unusual thing in the middle of a sentence. He asked, "Don't you ever wear jeans? Do you have something against them or what?"

"No," I responded, a tad defensively. I had gone to great lengths to always wear a nice long skirt or dress when I knew I was going to see him. I wanted to look the epitome of femininity. Now I began to wonder if he didn't like the way I looked. What was his problem? I thought I looked pretty good; conservative, feminine... Wait a minute, maybe he wanted to see me in jeans to see if I could be tough enough for farm life. Maybe he just wanted to check out my bum. Now, I was getting even more steamed. Then I remembered. I certainly had no problem checking out his bum in a pair of jeans, that first day we met. I got over myself, asked a quick silent prayer of forgiveness as I followed him to the car. My gaze dropped down to his bum. Yep, still cute, even in a pair of dress pants.

He drove me back to the church when we finished and hugged me good-bye. He didn't say, "I'll call you, I'll see you, or we'll get together again..." Nothing firm, just a bland "see ya later!"

"Lord, now what?" This was absolutely the last excuse I had to see him. "He doesn't date women (I wouldn't ask him out even if he did), and there are no more events to attend where I could run into him. What should I do?"

"Send him one of your headshots and write on it, 'Do black jeans count?' Tell him you still want to go out and pick corn," Was that you, God, or me?

My most recent shot was taken in L.A., one of those full body shots where I'm sitting on the ground, my arms holding my knees as I smile into camera. I'm wearing a pair of black jeans.

"You want me to do what, God? Sure. That's a billboard sign saying, 'Hi, I like you. Do you like me?' An 8 x 10 of me!"

At first I thought this was a ridiculous notion. I wasn't even sure if I had my headshots with me. I mean, I was already working; it wasn't like I needed them with me for auditions. They were probably in storage back in New York.

I went home and, out of curiosity, I began looking through my drawers for jeans. I really hadn't been wearing jeans too much since I had arrived; most of my stuff was workout clothes for rehearsals, or clothes for church. I pulled down my old suitcases from the closet, just to see if I'd left a pair or two in them. I did not find jeans, but I DID find headshots! Yes, my headshot in the black jeans was still inside a pocket of my suitcase. (That Karri had thought of everything!)

Fine, God, I'll do it and if I make a fool of myself, it's Your fault." I got the envelope ready, wrote the note on the headshot, sealed it up, and placed it on the dresser. I told myself if he didn't call that night, I'd mail it in the morning.

He didn't call me Sunday night as I had hoped he would. My thinking was that he would drive home, not able to get me off his mind, and that he would just have to call me and say what a wonderful time he had just had. Not exactly what he was thinking, because there was no call.

Chapter 10

The Gift of Light

Monday, August 14, 1995

Father, thank You for my time with Arlin yesterday. Lord, it was so neat how You sent his worker to go and do his work on Sunday so he could enjoy his afternoon talking to me over lunch. Thank You for Your financial provision to me so I could supply lunch. Thank You for Your support to pay all my bills. When I'm motivated out of love and desire, Lord, people get the best of me. But when I'm made to do something, I rebel. Father, I drove away from church after Arlin dropped me off and said, "That's my husband I just had lunch with."

Father, he's so much like me in that he loves his life with You. He loves how You have made him and what You are doing in him, and he desires to be free to have You solely. He said it would be humbling to know he 'needed anyone besides Jesus.' Lord, I told him I need people, I need fellowship, hugs, to be touched. That I can't do without this. But a husband...no, I can live—and have for thirty-seven years— without this. I desire a husband, but not one who clings to me out of desperation. Instead, let it be out of Your command to leave mother and father and cleave to one another. It seems as if he could fill a hole in my life and that he could love me with an open hand. I need that, Lord, so I can be free to move with You as I have.

Father, I ask that You speak to Arlin. Show him Proverbs 18:22: "He who finds a wife finds what is good and receives favor from the Lord." And show him his need for me, and that it's not to the detriment of his relationship with You. Give him Your purpose and design for us to come together. Anything less and it's a waste of time. Lord, I love You and for the first time in forever I see Your hand of glory in my life in the area of romance! I really am made to love a man on this earth, I feel that now. How wonderful are Your works in me! Continue to move me toward You and help me to cling to You as moss on a rock. Do not let the waves of the enemy wash me away. Guide me and protect me all the days of my life.

On Monday, I went to Mount Joy to mail my headshot, so he would receive it on Tuesday. Then I went back home, sat by the phone and waited. This was ridiculous! I jerked up the phone, and then put it back down. A minute later, I picked it back up. I began to dial. I needed encouragement…to do nothing! I called my friend Becky out in L.A. and cried, "Becky, what do I do now? He didn't mention anything about seeing me again or anything like he was remotely interested."

"Deb," she said, "If he's the man of God you say he is, God will tell *him* and he will make the next move. God will tell Arlin what to do. Now you just have to pray and wait." Great. One of my favorite things to do was to wait. And one of my most admirable attributes was patience. Yeah, right.

The next two days were excruciating. But I knew I couldn't sit by the phone forever. Our afternoon dance class was cancelled, but I did have a show that night, so I headed up to the bathroom to take a shower.

As I was getting out of the shower, I heard voices outside, below my upstairs window. I peeked out and looked down. There was Arlin! He was talking to my handyman, Galen (Yvonne's brother-in-law.) I jerked my head back in, out of sight, and quickly towel dried my hair. I ran to the bedroom and pulled…some new jeans (I finally found a pair folded up in the top of my closet)! I dashed down the steps, missing a few along the way. Then, took a deep breath and calmly, as casual as possible, opened my front door. I was just in time to see Arlin's car pulling away…with him in it!

I couldn't believe it. Why would he stop by and talk to the handyman and not even come by to see me. Then my mind started doing a simple family tree. Oh, my gosh! Galen is Yvonne's brother-in-law and Arlin is Yvonne's nephew… Holy cow (no pun intended): Galen must be Arlin's father!

The front porch door swung shut behind me as I approached Galen. I smiled, making small talk and then, nonchalantly, I asked, "So, is Arlin your son?" "Yes" he said. *Revelation!* Now I was really angry. Arlin stopped by to see his dad and didn't even have the courtesy to knock on my front door and drop in for one minute to say hello. That jerk! At that point, I really couldn't stand him.

Despite the fact I wanted to kill Arlin for being so rude and rejecting me, I heard this come out of my mouth: "Oh, you have such a nice son, such a wonderful man of God!" *Yuck! Did I really just say that?*

"Yeah, he's quite a fine Christian man. His mother did a good job," he said.

"Oh I think *you* did a wonderful job as his father," I said and went back in my house.

The phone rang. "What are you doing home? You're not supposed to be home. You're supposed to be at class!" It was Arlin calling from his cell phone.

"Uh…our instructor is on holiday for two weeks…"

"Well, I have something for you, but I didn't have the guts to leave it with… while you were there. Hurry up and leave and I'll come back by," he said.

Instantly, I was ashamed of myself! I quickly assured him I would be leaving within a half hour. I hung up the phone and dashed around the house picking up my make-up bag and grabbing my purse before racing out the door.

I rushed by Galen, "Bye," I blurted out with a quick wave and then jumped into my car. As I drove out of the driveway, I had an 'Aha moment.' Arlin wasn't just nervous about seeing me, he was also nervous about seeing his dad. When he pulled into my driveway and got out of his truck and saw his father around the side of my house working, he must have had to do some fast talking to not let on the real reason for stopping by my place.

Arlin's dad used to be a dairy farmer. Arlin bought the business from him when his dad retired, and his dad took up carpentry as a hobby. Until that day, I didn't know that this man working on my house was Arlin's father. I knew he was Yvonne's brother-in-law and that Arlin was her nephew, but I never put two and two together.

I'm sure Arlin didn't want his father to figure out why he had come by The Camp Woods nor why he was leaving something for the girl who lived in the house where his father was working. Arlin must have stopped dead in his tracks and quickly made an excuse for coming by. Mennonites traditionally do not believe in remarriage and the mere thought of Arlin having an interest in *any* woman was out of the question. For all anyone knew, he would remain single until he went home to be with the Lord. As I thought this through, I realized the huge risk Arlin was taking to engage in any kind of relationship with me; I admired him all the more.

I drove to the theatre; I couldn't stop smiling, nor could I stop agonizing over the thought of what he could possibly be dropping off at my house. Why did he want to *leave* something rather than give it to me in person? Though I got to the theatre and into wardrobe and make-up, my mind was on my front porch.

I couldn't stop thinking about what he might have left for me. I was more and more anxious and excited as the hours passed. Usually, performing in the show was the highlight of my day, but tonight, I couldn't wait for it to be over so I could get home.

Finally, I was in the car and on my way home. I knew the winding roads by heart and I usually enjoy listening to some uplifting music on the way home or I just open the windows and sing to God, just to feel the breeze in my hair and to give thanks for the beautiful drive.

But tonight, I buckled up and held the steering wheel tight. My prayers were only vain ones for no cops to see me cruise more than a few miles above the speed limit. After an eternity, I turned into The Camp Woods. As I curved around the path to my little cottage, I strained to see if I could make out any kind of package on the porch. I couldn't. It was too dark. I was in such a hurry to get away; I'd forgotten to turn on the porch light.

I slammed the car door closed and ran to the front porch steps, taking them two by two. The keys were out before I reached the front door. Reaching in, I tuned on the porch light and looked around frantically to look for what Arlin had left me. There on the wicker table beside the rocker was a funny looking gun-looking thing with a pretty ribbon and a card attached to the top. I quickly snatched it up, plopped myself into the rocker and began to read: *Dear Deborah, here's something to help light up your time with Jesus. Thank you for the lunch and wonderful fellowship on Sunday. 1 Corinthians 13. Arlin.*

I picked up the 'gun' thingy and began playing with it. Eventually I got it to light. At first I was puzzled and then I giggled, remembering our conversation at brunch.

Before we had left the restaurant, I had asked the waitress for matches. He was somewhat surprised at my request and asked if I smoked. "No," I said, "I collect matches to light my candles when I have my candlelight baths with Jesus."

He asked, "Don't you have one of those automatic lighter things?"

"No," I said, "I have never seen one." So, that was the gift he bought to go with the card. He tied a pretty ribbon around it and placed it on the table on the porch with the card.

But, what was the "1 Corinthians 13" supposed to mean? On the cover of the black and white card were a little girl and boy swinging together. I knew 1 Corinthians 13 was the love chapter in the Bible, but it could mean love as in a Christian brother and sister or romantic love. Which did he mean?

I had to know, or at least attempt to figure it out. I called him immediately and thanked him for the gift and the card. Then I asked if he'd like to drop by for coffee that evening. He said yes he would! That meant he'd be coming alone to my house without any bodyguards. Oh no, things were becoming very interesting, very fast.

He had just finished working on the farm and said he had to shower and dress, but that he would be over shortly. I thought that meant half an hour.

One and one half hours later he shows up! I was dying of suspense the entire time. He took his time once again, I imagine to keep me in suspense and to maintain his indecipherable intentions.

I had no idea what to say when he got to my house or what was going to happen. I prayed… desperately. "God, I need a little help here. This man is coming over to my house, minus the bodyguards, and he just gave me this card and gift. What does all this mean? He's a man that doesn't think he needs anyone, doesn't want to be married, doesn't date, and now he's coming over to my house… alone. Hello!"

Arlin walked up, politely said hi, and sat down on the rocker in the corner on the porch. I had been sitting there, waiting, trying to appear casual and unflustered. When we talked, I could tell he was nervous; thank God because so was I. He evidently had something he wanted to tell me, but he was having a bit of a struggle verbalizing just what it was.

But then, a calm confidence overtook him, and a two-hour interrogation began. The Arlin Inquisition; he asked me to start from the time I was five years old and go through my entire life *one* year at a time, telling him the best and worst thing that happened each year. How dare he ask such personal questions; how stupid was I to answer?!

I began, as he requested, at the age of five. Two hours later, I was getting tired of my own stories, assuming he was, too. Many times I tried to skip a few years here and there without him noticing because I wasn't sure how old he was, but I knew I was older. I didn't want him to figure out how much older.

He would catch me advancing the years and say, "Oh no, no, no… Go back to when you were eleven. Now tell me the most wonderful thing and the worst thing that happened to you at that age." I couldn't believe it! At first I felt annoyed at his persistence, then flattered at his attentiveness, and then annoyed again: where was this going? I finally said, "Okay, okay. Enough already! Time to hear about you!" Finally, he began to talk.

He was stumbling over his words a bit. I couldn't make out what he was trying to say. Then, he stopped for a moment, and began to tentatively plow ahead. He said, "You know, I have a hard time expressing myself. When I don't sense the anointing of God, I just can't express myself. It's too hard. I had something I wanted to tell you, but I don't sense the anointing anymore—so I can't say it." Poor guy. He was scared to death. Anointing…shmointing! I told him to go ahead and say whatever was on his mind.

So, he told me this *long* story about going to Mardi Gras with a street preacher and how this girl on the trip had fallen in love with him. As I was listening to this *long*, drawn-out story, I asked myself, "And what does this have to do with the price of rice in China?"

We had walked off the porch and were sitting on the tailgate of his truck by now. It was a full moon, a beautiful evening, and this guy is telling me about some girl who had the hots for him in New Orleans? I was *not* getting it.

When we first sat down on the tailgate, he momentarily interrupted himself to ask me what I was doing there on a night like this, with a full moon, and with him.

"I'm here, in Landisville, because I'm being obedient to God because this is the *last* place on earth I expected be! I'm here with you, because… Well, why don't you tell me why I'm here with you," I replied.

He smiled at me and brushed his hand across my cheek, which gave me the sweetest tingle down my spine. "I hoped this day would come someday, but I thought it would be eight or ten years into the future."

He returned to his story and proceeded to tell me that he actually felt sorry for this girl because he had no interest in her. He was actually put off that she didn't have *total* focus on Jesus while they were on a mission. At that point in his story, he says that's when the Lord nailed him. He showed him she had the better portion. She was willing to love.

Okay, side note; I *totally* was not getting it here! What was his point? I figured he was about to say, "So, I get the sense that you like me, kind of like she did, and…well, I don't have any interest in you. We'll just be friends. But it's mighty admirable of you to risk rejection and all," or some crazy thing like that. The *ax* was coming—or so I thought…

Chapter 11

Is This Really Happening?

The ax didn't come at all. What happened instead was his confession:"I was on my knees for one hour at the Bible study last night trying to get you out of my mind so I could hear from God. The Lord said, 'Arlin, why can't you love? Why don't you just let go and love?' I knew what I had to do." Then he looked intently at me and continued. "I don't care about being a fool for you or Christ, or being humbled by God. I don't care if I make a fool out of myself right now. Can I tell you that I love you and I want you to be my wife?"

What?

Now I was speechless. (That in itself was a minor miracle.) I wasn't sure what to say next. So, I said, "Do you know how old I am?"

"Yes."

"And that doesn't bother you?"

"No." He answered. "Do you know how old I am and do you have a problem with that?"

"No," I said, still awe struck with that 'deer in the headlights' kind of stare.

But, actually, I had no idea what age he was. I just knew he was younger— but I didn't know by how much. It turned out he was six years younger!

Funny how things work out…Two years earlier at a wedding reception in New York City, I was sitting next to a friend of mine talking about the various couples around our table. Wesley, one of my best friends, and I were the only singles at the table. A woman sitting with us was a mutual acquaintance with her new husband, five years her junior.

I leaned over and whispered to Wesley, "I would *never* marry a younger man. Only desperate women had to marry younger men." *Ouch!* That was a large foot-in-mouth. Just like the time ten years earlier when I went horseback-riding with a friend who lived in a mobile home out in the country.

I remember telling God that I would *never* live in a mobile home! I felt sorry for my friend. Now, if I were to take this proposal seriously, my future would include a single- wide mobile home...on a beautiful piece of property overlooking incredible pasture land and a babbling brook—living forever with a very Godly, handsome, kind-hearted...younger dairy farmer.

Back to what was becoming my reality. After the initial *monumental* shock of Arlin's sudden marriage proposal—I said, "Let's take a walk." I needed to breathe, and think and *beg* God to have me stay calm as I processed what was happening. We took a walk around The Camp Woods, and I am sure I appeared very calm as I told my legs to slowly take one step in front of the other, but my heart was racing with excitement. I began to explain everything I had been going through mentally and emotionally, since meeting him. I detailed my feelings, hesitations and hopes over the course of the previous two weeks up until this moment. I shared with him everything I had written in my journal, including my conversations with God over this whole strange and wonderful time.

We arrived back at the cottage just as I was finishing and I said, "All that to say, I believed you were my husband since the day we met. I was just waiting for God to show *you* that, too. Now that He has...*yes*, I'll marry you!" His smile was all I needed.

Everything in me was screaming. *Can this be the* real *thing?! After 17 years of praying for a husband, this is it! He is the one! I can't believe he just asked and I said yes!* His smile was all I needed to reassure me: Yes! This was real.

Naturally, all I wanted to do was kiss him, but we hadn't even held hands yet! I was afraid to get near him before. Neither did I want him to know I had any interest. Who wants to suffer rejection?

"I don't think we should get rings right away," he said. "And, I don't think we should even kiss."

"Well, you got the marriage part right and possibly the ring part, but to not even kiss for one year, you *definitely* got that one wrong." I leaned over to kiss him and that was it. Really, now we were engaged—and in my mind, kissing was within bounds. In fact, we stood next to his pickup from midnight to 2 a.m. kissing!

I didn't want to let him go. I guess he didn't either because he wanted to go to the justice of the peace *that* weekend and get married right away. Of course, I said no. I wanted the *grand* wedding I had been dreaming of for 17 years. The one with the gazillion bridesmaids, the organ playing as I walked down the aisle of a big, beautiful historic cathedral with marble floors, lots of statues and art, the big cake, tons of people, and of course all the showers, parties, shopping galas—the whole nine yards. I had been a bridesmaid one too many times. And, now it was my turn; I was not going to miss out. I could fill a room with all those ridiculous, stomach turning 'one-of-a-kind' dresses! Now it was my turn.

That was my first big mistake. I should have opted for his plan, the justice of the peace, and ditched the diva scene. My life would have been much less complicated…

Chapter 12

Yes, It's Really Happening

Arlin had been married at a very young age. His marriage was not forced or totally arranged, but he was persuaded to marry a young lady, whom he had been seeing since he was 15 and whose family was ex-Amish, Shortly before their formal engagement, he had gone to his mother and told her he didn't want to marry her. Again, he was persuaded to move forward with the marriage. In Lancaster, almost everyone is related. The majority marry within the culture, as it's part of the Mennonite/Amish tradition to marry within their own faith and culture. That's understandable; it keeps things simple.

Funny thing, I always wanted to marry a foreigner. And it looked like I was about to if I married Arlin. He just happened to be from the United States! Never in my life, or in all my travels abroad, had I ever experienced a more closed-off, exclusive community than in Lancaster, Pennsylvania!

After much convincing from his family, Arlin married the girl. Seven years later, his wife ran off with another man. Technically, at least according to his church, he was innocent because she left him. Still, divorce was not accepted in this community, or if it was, it wasn't without those looks of, "Oh, *he's divorced!* And did you hear what happened?" *Blah, blah, blah…*

The divorce, however, was what led to Arlin's conversion experience with God. It was during this event in his life that He became "born-again." Everything old in his life died. Now, after surrender to Christ, Arlin had a new life. He was still in his 20s, and still very much a part of the Mennonite community, if for nothing else, for his family's sake. So, would he now be shunned from the community because of his divorce? How would his family and church treat him? There had never been divorce in his family before this, but in keeping with Mennonite customs, it was clear that his family assumed that he would never remarry.

Arlin realized that up until that point in time, he had just been religious. He had a mental assent to a "god" out there, but he had never had a *heart* conversion, he had just plain, old 'fire insurance.' He had never met Jesus; he only knew about Him. Sure, he had gone up to the altar many times for the traditional altar call because, given the choice of "burn in hell forever" or say these words and live blissfully in heaven with God, what would any rational human being choose? Altar time! That's a no-brainer.

Before Arlin gave his life to Christ, his gods had been money, power, and reputation. Now, in one stroke, those were all removed. But, by having a divorce, Arlin opened himself up to criticism. He should have had to wear the letter *D* on his chest, like Hester with the letter A on hers in *The Scarlet Letter.* And so began his true journey with the Lord.

About the same time, a close friend of his, Lamar, also experienced a real conversion. For the next two years, they went together to Bible studies and praise worship services almost every night to soak up the things of God, seeking out those who had the "real" Jesus. The two of them were on an adventure, *Starsky and Hutch style;* without the tight jeans and bad hair. (If you don't remember the show – Google it, just for a laugh!)

For the first time in his life, Arlin had a real relationship with Jesus Christ! At the same time, members of his family and others in the Mennonite Church told him he could never remarry. He would have to be celibate for the rest of his life. He wanted to honor his family, but something about this teaching seemed a little…off. The God he was learning about was one of forgiveness and freedom. Arlin had owned up to his part in the marriage; he had listened to his family rather than his conscience. He had repented and was ready to move on with God and His direction. But something was holding him back; the legality and constraints of his upbringing. Arlin's family didn't purposefully misguide him, but they were misinterpreting the scripture on the marriage issue and it all became very confusing.

About three months before we met, Arlin attended a revival in Toronto. He heard one amazing message about God's grace, and the message cleared his mind about the question of remarriage. He discovered the grace of God meant he *could* remarry, if he chose to and if God was directing him to do so. He had grown up with a gospel of works, but was now experiencing and hearing something new: the *true* gospel of grace.

God's perfect timing. Now Arlin was ready for God to bring his wife into his life, the one intended for him from the foundation of time. He was waiting, like I was, for the one who was meant to be with him forever, bone of bone and flesh of flesh.

Now the hard part: Arlin slowly started to tell his family he was getting remarried. First, he told his parents and then his siblings and close friends. News traveled fast throughout the community, and, just as quickly, the opposition began to pour in. They had no idea he was even seeing anyone, much less getting married!

When I began this adventure, I had no idea that this community was so close-knit. You don't need a telephone around here; word travels, as if blown across the tops of corn fields from farm to farm. The onslaught of negative responses and inappropriate tirades began. Arlin received phone calls from people who begged him not to marry me. He received letters saying that he would go to hell and lose his salvation if he were to remarry. He spared me of all the wonderful details for a while, but soon enough I found out what was happening and I was devastated. Here I was, going through the biggest transition of my life and hoping for a welcoming embrace from the community—which I had grown to love—to make this change go smoothly. Instead I was practically shunned and put into the awkward position of having to defend myself. I also felt extremely burdened for Arlin.

After all, this was his home. He deserved to be treated with the respect he had earned over the years. Instead he was judged and labeled; all as a result of choosing me. I felt guilty, but simultaneously proud of him. He was standing up for what he believed in; he was taking up this cause… for me! He was truly my knight in shining armor and I fell even more deeply in love with him.

Speaking of my being a princess, back in Texas, my mother 'the queen,' was in the throes of planning a grand wedding for Arlin and me. By the end of October, she had sent out 400 invitations! The date was set for December 9th. My worlds were beginning to collide, yet again.

Chapter 13

Encounters

In September, Arlin and I made plans to fly to Texas so he could meet my parents and formally ask for my hand in marriage. Needless to say, I was nervous for him to meet my clan. I mean, there's a reason why I'm a "take no prisoners, loud-mouthed, say-it-like-it-is-whether-you-like-it-or-not," kind of gal. I grew up with a family the same way: we're *Italian*.

We grew up in the typical Italian, Roman Catholic family, full of emotion, lots of screaming and lots of drama…quite different from Arlin's Mennonite home where absolutely no one *ever* raised their voice or, God forbid, *cursed*, or showed any emotion!

What would Arlin think of my family? Perhaps we're all *nuts?!*

The day we were to fly out to Texas, Arlin came to pick me up at 6 a.m. to take me for coffee before I left for the theatre. I thought it a bit funny that he wanted to come over so early to have coffee with me when we would be sitting on the plane together that afternoon for five hours, but, whatever. I forgot to leave the front door open and didn't set my alarm, so I was still sleeping when he came to get me.

He threw rocks at my second-story window and called out to me to wake me up. It was Saturday, the day we had four shows in a row. The theatre had given me off the last two shows of the day so I could fly home Saturday and return Tuesday in time for the shows that day. The theatre was closed Sunday and Monday. Finally, I heard the rocks against my window.

Earlier in August, right after Arlin had proposed to me, we discussed wedding rings. I didn't know that most traditional Mennonites didn't have rings, or for that matter, they didn't wear jewelry at all. It was considered too worldly. His parents don't have rings. He asked me what I wanted in a ring. Now, where I came from, Texas, and more recently, New York City, let's just say, there ain't no problem with jewelry. Almost everything my girlfriends, sisters, and sisters-in-law were sporting was *big*, as in *diamonds*. That's what I was accustomed to. No big deal.

I didn't know Arlin's financial situation, though, so I decided to refrain from saying what I wanted, or had envisioned. It wasn't exactly at the top of the list of things I was concerned about at the time. I was thinking dress; bridesmaids' dresses; place; food; music; and invitation lists *A, B,* and *C.* I had entered full bride mode! The ring was his department.

Later, Arlin called my sister in New York City who put him in touch with a friend of ours who's a diamond broker in the city. David informed Arlin that I wanted three carats. I can only imagine Arlin's response on the phone; most likely silence, shock, and then rage. It was actually a little less intense. Arlin was shocked, surprised, and then angry. He came right over to my house and read me the riot act about materialism and blah, blah, *blah*. I guess some of the Mennonite was still in him.

I was furious and said, "Look, I told David, in a casual conversation, that I thought three carats would be nice, *someday.* That was years ago and I wasn't even seeing anyone! I didn't say I *had to* have three carats! It was something I just always dreamed of." Then I took a deep breath and looked into his eyes. I could see all he wanted to do was please me. I softly added, "It's not a big deal. For that matter, forget the rings. We don't have to have rings. I'm not letting our relationship be ruined over a stupid thing like rings. Forget the rings. Okay?" He took my hand and kissed it. That was the last I heard about rings.

Back to our 6 a.m. coffee date, I came downstairs, freshly dressed, and got into his car. We drove to another farm nearby, which his family owned. There was a beautiful, huge lawn out front all set up for a polo match. We drove down the long driveway toward an old red brick farmhouse. I was wondering why we were going to this farm. Did he need to check on a cow?

We then pulled up to the barn in the back and he said, "Okay, get out."

"'Okay, get out'? What do you mean get out? Where are we going?"

He came around the side, blindfolded me with his hands, and led me through what felt like a field of tall grass. Then he took his hands down.

"Okay, now you can look," he said.

About one hundred feet away was his truck in the middle of acres of beautiful green grass shining brilliantly with the morning sunrise! The back of the truck was laid out with a red and white checkered picnic cloth, a breakfast full of my favorite breakfast foods—cereal, blueberry muffins, fruit, orange juice, coffee, and fresh milk—all on china, crystal, and silver. *And* a red rose in a crystal vase right in the middle of it all. I was astonished. What a fun ride

I'm on with this incredibly surprising man! For a Mennonite farm boy, *he's doing pretty well!*

He guided me over to the back of his truck. As we reached the beautiful picnic he had created, he got down on one knee, pulled out a black box, opened it, and asked me to marry him *again*. In the box was the most beautiful (not quite three-carat) diamond ring with sapphire trillions I had ever seen! I actually heard myself gasp; this was definitely big-screen kind of stuff!

I was literally blown away! This couldn't be real. What happened? I thought we had agreed there would be no rings? And this fabulous breakfast, served on crystal and china, all for me? I felt like I was dreaming and at any moment I would just have to wake up. But I was fully awake and present in the moment and so was God. He had created exactly this moment for me; how amazing! Arlin was such an incredible gift, one I didn't expect or even dream of ever getting. As I looked into his eyes at that moment, I was determined to do all I could to make him feel like I was a gift for him, as well.

Arlin's timing was impeccable. That afternoon we got on our flight, with my beautiful ring gleaming from sunlight shining through the airplane window. It's true what they say: when you are wearing the ring given to you by the one you are going to be with forever, you can't stop staring at it! I must have looked at my hand 20 times an hour. I simply couldn't help myself.

My parents were simply taken with Arlin. They could see instantly why I fell in love with him. His 'down home,' earnest charm juxtaposed with his business savvy (and of course, in their opinion, his impeccable taste in choosing their daughter) was a winning combination! And yes, they liked the ring. They're living in Texas; big was definitely better!

Our engagement party was spectacular; everything my heart had dreamed of. We were having a wonderful visit. But then there were the usual family squabbles that were inevitable, just by the sheer nature of the fact that there were more than two of us in a room. Arlin's head was spinning from the range of emotion displayed in a five-minute interlude.

On the plane home, he described my family: "It's unbelievable. One minute they're screaming at each other at the top of their lungs, the next minute they're asking each other where they're meeting for lunch and at what time, like they're best friends and nothing ever happened! I've never seen *heathens* act this way, much less Christians!" Okay, so my family is a little... how do we say...*loud?* We get it all out, we get over it, and we move on. That's healthy isn't it? Anyway, he'll get used to it, I hoped.

Sunday, October 1, 1995

I have not written the events of my life for awhile—but so many unbelievable things have happened! Lord, You are so changing my life and my heart. You are moving me here to Mount Joy. I remember when You said when I returned to New York from Europe last September a year ago, "Don't plant your feet. Your vision is too small. I am expanding your vision." But, I never expected that would mean a move to Lancaster, and I never expected what Your whole reason for bringing me here was. It is so clear to me now, You can open doors—but only You.

Chapter 14

Intervention

Arlin and I went to New York City at the end of September to meet with my pastor and get his approval of Arlin. Tim Keller is one of the most incredible men of God I have ever known. Tim was kind of like my New York City father figure, and I really wanted to have him meet Arlin, so they could get to know one another. Arlin and I met with him for a couple of hours and I had a great time as we told our story and he asked questions.

During this trip, Arlin and I had our first head-on encounter with the enemy. We were strolling down Fifth Avenue Saturday afternoon and Arlin began saying that I didn't tell the truth; I added things here and there. He began to say that I greatly exaggerated and, because he felt that I *embellished,* he began to question everything I said. Had he forgotten I was Italian?!

The fact that I might "embellish" from time to time did not make me a liar. I was livid! Now, looking back, I have to admit, I was not ready to admit that I exaggerated—or should I say "embellished"—any of my stories. He had just accused me of making everything up! I couldn't handle that kind of accusation from a man who was going to become my husband. It made me all the more defensive.

Okay, where was all that training on how the enemy divides?

I immediately told him that I thought Satan was trying to put doubts in his mind and pit us against one another. I knew that God had put us together for His glory and Satan hates that. Our relationship was not your typical "boy meets girl" scenario. I was convinced that God went to great lengths to put us together. Why would the enemy just lie down and say, "Hey, knock yourselves out!" *No!* He comes to steal, kill, and destroy! By that evening, Arlin agreed it was probably the enemy placing doubts in his mind. I was relieved and I thought that was the end of it.

Less than a month later, he freaked out again. The calls, letters, and visits from friends and family urging him to call off our wedding were continuing to pour in and fuel doubt in his mind. How could our marriage be right with God if not one person he knew approved of this relationship? Well, there was one lone ranger that stood with him, and that was his mother, Eileen. She had seen the change in her son since his divorce and his conversion. She believed, since Arlin said God told him to marry me, Arlin should marry me. But she stood alone in her support of him and our upcoming marriage.

This time when Arlin had doubts, he said he didn't want to talk to me or see me for a couple of days so he could think through things. I was devastated, not sure what this meant for our future together.

Tuesday, October 17, 1995

Father in heaven, I thank You for Your glorious provision of Jesus Christ without whom I would have no hope. Thank You for Your Holy Spirit that indwells me and thank You for Your Word that today in my hour of pain and sorrow feeds my soul and brings comfort to my spirit. Thank You, God, that You love me no matter what, that You will never leave me or forsake me, nor will You penalize me for my weaknesses, sins, and mistakes. Father, why does Arlin feel a need to hurt me purposefully—to withdraw and make me pay for this disagreement? He is Your son, You made him, fearfully and wonderfully, according to Your plan. Help me to understand him. Give me the grace and mercy to love him the way You do—to help him through his struggles. Help me to be courageous enough to tell him the truth in love and endure the pain when he lashes out at me in defense. God, I thank You that You are always there and I can run to You with this hurt. Why, Lord, does he take the very delicate things of my heart that I share in vulnerability and openness and use them against me in his anger?" I am trying, Lord. Do forgive me for my sin in my anger toward Your son, Arlin. I do feel as though I hate him when he refuses to see the truth and walks away from communicating. I thank You, though, now and forever, for the gift of him whom You have given me. I know You only give good gifts. In the spirit I know he is a man after Your own heart; I believe this Lord. Thank You, for Your grace has poured out on me abundantly. May Your grace and mercy and love pour out on Arlin in abundance.

Father, I do not want to be a stumbling block to this man in his walk with You. It is so easy when we separate ourselves from relationships—there are no problems, but we don't grow. There's no accountability; there's no truth being spoken into our lives. The tendency is to walk around deceived because when one is the strongest, that one has no accountability, no one to call them and encourage them into the high calling of Christ Jesus. We become complacent in our walk, believing we have mastered the faith. God, thank You for the Pauls and Timothys

You have placed in my life and for the spiritual mothers You have put in my path who are willing to speak honestly into my life without fear of rejection. I thank You for all those who have suffered me unto themselves as I struggled through areas of sin, deception, unbelief, doubt, and weakness. Thank You for Your men who have loved me unconditionally for the past fifteen years—who have held my hands and walked with me. God, I do not take for granted these gifts, but I am sad. I see they can no longer be my confidants as in the past. That now has to shift to Arlin—the man You have predestined from the foundations for me. I am still so blown away at how You creatively brought me to Lancaster to unite me with him—to put me before him. Lord Jesus, thank You for being so creative. I love Your ways! I don't understand them, but I love them nonetheless. Jesus, You have been such a wonderful husband—perfect—and now I must turn to Your leading in and through this man. I am fearful—not of Your will, but of his flesh. Help me not to run, but to endure the pain, the arrows at my heart, and the false accusations straight from the pit of hell. You called me to this and I know You will see me through. "Live in peace with each other. And we urge you, brothers, warn those who are idle, encourage the timid, help the weak, and be patient with everyone. Make sure that nobody pays back wrong for wrong, but always try to be kind to each other and to everyone else. Be joyful always, pray continually, and give thanks in all circumstances for this is God's will for you in Jesus Christ." Read 1 Thessalonians 5:16–18.

It had been two full days since Arlin and I had spoken. I went to the farm the next night to find Arlin working in the barn. He sent me to his house to wait for him to finish. He arrived looking irritated and exhausted. We sat down on his couch and began to talk through what was happening and what we were going to do about it. He was feeling confused by all the pressure he was receiving. At the same time, some of my faults were beginning to show. It scared him. We prayed together and asked God to be a part of this time in our lives, to weed out confusion, and to be with us in times of doubt. Neither one of us felt very comforted at that moment, but out of obedience, we agreed to move forward and ignore everyone else. We decided to continue to pray together and seek God for guidance and help. And, oh glory, I was about to need both!

Arlin called me the next morning and said his sister wanted to meet with me.

"What? Why do I have to meet with her?"

"She just wants to meet with you and talk to you," he said. "Listen, Deborah, you really have to go. She is insistent."

"What do you mean 'she is insistent'? And what the heck is this all about? I don't owe her any explanation; our relationship is none of her business. What could she possibly have to say to me about anything?"

"Just go, Deborah," he answered. "You really need to just meet with her. I don't know what she wants to say, but you do need to go."

That truly made me angry. Who was she; the town's spokesperson or the grand Poobah of the family? Did she have a right to *demand* I meet with her? She hadn't done anything to get to know me. She failed to call me herself to request this meeting. She was requiring this meeting, but not able to call me directly? It was as if she were some ruler of an imaginary kingdom, summoning me through one of her subjects. I did NOT have to bow down to this request!

Okay, I went. It was cold and rainy that afternoon. She, her husband, and three-year-old daughter were living in the apartment-side of the farmhouse, that winter. Her father was in the process of building her a house. I drove down to the farm dressed in my black leather skirt and jacket with black leggings and knee-high black leather boots. This was not New York City, but I was 'representin' and I wanted her to know it! We sat down at her kitchen table.

She was dressed simply enough in khaki pants and a pressed white button down shirt. Her face seemed calm, but an arched eyebrow and a hint of a twitch in her left eye said differently. Finally, while pouring tea, she spoke. "What are you going to do if you marry Arlin and none of us accept you? And none of us talk to you or decide to be your friend? What will you do, up on the hill all alone with no friends or family?" she said.

I think, at that point, *my* eye began to twitch. *Are you kidding?!* I thought with my mouth agape. Who does this woman think she is; the grand madam of Mount Joy?! I was in such disbelief that she actually thought she could intimidate me into calling off the wedding and returning to New York. Actually, I was in shock!

Finally, I said, "You know what? I'm not marrying you *or* this family. I'm marrying Arlin. If you have a problem with me, that's *your* tough luck. I have enough friends and family for a lifetime; I don't need *any* of you!" I exclaimed.

I got up and walked out. I actually felt rejuvenated; a slight smile crossed my face as I slammed the door of Arlin's truck. My high-top leather boots pressed the pedal to the metal and I sped away with new resolve to marry this man whether his family or the whole town, for that matter, wanted me to or not!

Chapter 15
Speaking My Mind

Thursday, October 19, 1995

Oh Father! What another glorious day! As I drove this morning, I saw Your beauty in the willow trees over the misty pond of a farm. Wow, God. Thank You for loving me enough to share that beauty with me. It reminds me of the mornings I went walking last September in the wine country of Italy at sunrise and how You said "Here I am" in the beauty of all the acres of vineyards and orchards of peaches, oranges, and plums amidst the mountainsides. And then the small, beautiful church at the top of the mountain. I remember, Lord. We made a beautiful memory that day. Father, last night was the toughest night of my life. Is that anything like what You felt when Peter betrayed You? Arlin totally betrayed me. You were there. You knew it was coming. Thank You for preparing me with a mindset of obedience and the discernment to understand it was Satan as he was speaking through Arlin. God, as I step out in radical trust and obedience in this relationship, I see the enemy lurks ever closer. Lead me to Your Word today to talk to me about You. Remind me again, Father, about who You are. Ignite my faith and build truth in my inward parts. I want to cling to You and never let anything like wedding plans deter me from You. Truly You do have stubborn love. You never quit drawing, calling, loving. Incredible. You are incredible. Will I ever attain that standard?

I was so thankful I had that time with the Lord. I needed the reassurance of His presence in my life as things were clearly going to get worse before they got any better. Knowing God was by my side allowed me to keep my sanity, no matter what was coming next.

The subsequent and unexpected meeting was a visit from his closest friend, Hoover. I had gone to Arlin's house one evening after I finished at the theatre and Hoover came over for what I thought would be a friendly, 'get to know you better' visit. But when we sat down in his living room, Hoover began his monologue; more of a rant, really.

"Arlin, what are you doing getting married? This cannot be the will of God! Please, Arlin, I'm begging you! Don't marry her. She's not right for you. Can't you see that? " And on and on he went. I was sitting right there next to Arlin, listening to all of this.

Okay, now what movie is this a flashback from? This can't really be happening. Doesn't he see me sitting here and doesn't he realize who he's speaking about? I can be gracious, but he's way over the top on this one.

Arlin didn't say a word. Should I have been surprised? Finally, as a last ditch effort, Hoover got on his knees, started crawling across the floor to Arlin, crying and begging him not to marry me and make 'the biggest mistake of his life.'

"She's just a desperate woman who wants a ring on her finger and a man! Please don't marry her, Arlin! Don't do it!"

I was watching this whole thing unfold before my eyes in utter amazement. If it hadn't been so strange, it would have been funny. This was the most desperate attempt I had seen, yet, to stop our wedding. This guy is a trucker? Clearly, he was in the wrong business, the casting directors for daytime 'soaps' would have loved this guy. And I thought *I* was a good actress!

"Arlin, this is ridiculous. Say something! I don't have to take this abuse— this guy is crazy!"

Thank God Arlin finally spoke up.

"Okay, Hoover, that's enough. This is getting a bit ridiculous. You'll have to leave now."

Hoover continued to cry, moan, and beg, insisting Arlin was making the biggest mistake of his life and that this relationship was a work of the devil. I'm telling you, Satan got a lot of credit on this one.

Finally, the drama ended. Arlin walked Hoover to his car, I guess to insure he actually got in it and drove away! I sat there in the silence of the trailer and began laughing. I mean, I couldn't stop! This was getting so crazy I had to just succumb to the insanity of it all. When Arlin came back in, I'm sure he thought he was going to find me brooding or crying or whatever. When he saw me, almost unable to control myself with giggles, he couldn't help but join in. His shoulders dropped and he seemed to relax for the first time in weeks.

Maybe Hoover was actually God's gift, after all. It was the closest I had felt to Arlin since we'd gotten engaged; funny how God can turn ugly into beautiful. Satan meant it for evil. God, as we should expect by now, made it good.

Chapter 16

World Meets World

The show closed at the end of October. My mother met us in New York City to help pack up my apartment and help me move my things to Arlin's trailer in Pennsylvania. Mom and I drove back down to Pennsylvania, and unloaded. That night mom and I stayed at the farm at Arlin's parents B&B. She met with his parents for the *first* time and inquired in her New York accent and to-the-point manner about how they felt knowing we were getting married. She asked whether or not they had any doubts or concerns about her daughter.

They said, "No." 'Right.'

The whole family was screaming at Arlin, "Don't do it!" but they weren't about to share that with my mother. Still, only Arlin's mother was supportive of the marriage. When Arlin told her that God had spoken to his heart about me, she believed him, understood, and trusted the Lord. She understood the things of God.

Mom and I left the next day for New York City. Two bridal showers were being thrown for me that week. I was so excited and was having all the usual bride jitters. I couldn't wait to celebrate with all my girlfriends in New York. I hadn't seen many of them in six months. It was party time! The plan was that after all the celebrations in New York, mom and I would fly to Texas until the wedding in December. It was now November 3rd.

The day after we arrived back in New York City on November 4, Arlin called and we had another argument. His family had approached him asking about the stories I had told them regarding my vision for the two of us. That was one of my biggest mistakes, sharing my dreams with people who couldn't understand the things of God.

Backing up a bit: In October, all the girls at the theatre had given me a shower. All the women in Arlin's family had refused to come and support me. At the last minute, his mom and one of his oldest sisters, the "grand madam" who had questioned me earlier, showed up. No one before that had come by to welcome me to the family, have me for tea or coffee, introduce themselves, get to know me, or even to meet me. Not even to say hello, how are you, congratulations, or drop dead. *Nothing!*

Arlin suggested that I take his two sisters, sisters-in-law, and mom out to brunch on Sunday to allow them to get to know me. I thought that was odd. Wasn't that their job? But, he said, "You're the believer. You have to extend your hand first." Clearly, he was right. I invited them. Amazingly, they accepted. Off to brunch it was.

They questioned me at brunch about my plans for Arlin and me. They wondered just what I thought Arlin and I were going to do after we were married. Well, I *had* been living in New York City and L.A. while working in the entertainment business. So it made sense I had thoughts and dreams of Arlin and me working with Steven Spielberg or other notable filmmakers doing amazing films of meaningful stories both fictional and biographical. If God's purpose for us was to spread the gospel and grow the kingdom, why not do it through the power of the media? This seemed perfectly reasonable to me.

Also, I had been temping for a major holding company with ties to the entertainment business before arriving in Pennsylvania. Many major players in the entertainment business frequented the townhouse where I worked. I had seen how easy it was for God to put me before the right people when He wanted to get His work done. I had the faith to believe in *anything* where God was concerned. He runs the world and everything in it! *He's* on the throne and in charge!

Not surprisingly, they all thought I was basically out of my mind. I should have known better. What could I have possibly been thinking? Look where it got Joseph in the Bible when he shared his dream with his eleven brothers. It got him sold into slavery, followed by the dungeon in Egypt. Nice…

Arlin had dinner with his family at the farm the day after I had returned to the city with my mom. They questioned him about my dreams and visions. He told them that they should take what I said, cut it in half, and only believe that much. He said I had a problem with exaggerating because I had the need to feel important. Basically, that I lived in la-la land, and perhaps I was hallucinating!

When he reiterated this conversation to me over the phone, adding "and *now* my family can love and accept you because they understand you have a *problem,"* I went through the roof! Yes, I did embellish at times to make the story better. For instance, "There were 500 people at the party" when in fact there were only 275 or something like that—*but* the party existed. I *never* made up stuff! In my mind, this was no big deal. What was his problem? I was boiling! *Now his family could accept me because they thought I was a basket case? And now what would I be, their new project?!*

"Forget you, Arlin, and the cow you rode in on! I take back everything I ever said to you!" I screamed over the phone to him. I called off the wedding; or maybe he did. I can't remember who said it first, the point was, we were no longer getting married, lovely.

The next two days were days of darkness. What happened, God? Did I miss You? Did Arlin miss You? He was receiving loads of pressure from everyone telling him he was making a *big* mistake. The bottom line was this: We were being tested and the enemy was coming in like the flood.

In the meantime, back in the city, mother could not stand to see me cry my guts out on the floor of my sister's apartment. At night, she cradled me in her arms and held me until I fell asleep. But I could tell it was getting to be too much for her. She hinted she needed to go back and I was more than willing for her to go. I didn't want her to see me like this as much as she didn't want to.

She was as confused and baffled as I was. Who were these people? What was wrong with Arlin? It was beyond her. She had genuinely grown to love him in such a short time. She too believed he was the answer to her prayers for her daughter, all these years. Now, what would happen? How could things turn around from here? Two days later, she booked a flight and returned to Texas.

My girlfriends and I met that night in lieu of the shower they had planned for me. They put me in a soft cozy chair in the middle of the room and began to counsel me. I asked them to tell me the truth. "Do I lie? Do I exaggerate, embellish, or make up stories?"

They loved me with the truth.

"No, Deb, you don't lie. But sometimes you leave out important details. Sometimes, it makes us feel as if you're the only one with the awesome God stories, and why don't they happen to us? You are an incredible gift of God to all of us, you just need to be more specific…and precise…when you tell your stories," they said.

We had a few glasses of wine and a great girl's night. Free therapy! We spent the next three days together, with them telling me, lovingly, the faults they saw in me—and with me humbly listening and absorbing it all. Then we prayed and asked God to change me. If anything or all of what Arlin or the girls said was true, I wanted to change. I was sure about this truth: that's how growth happens in the Lord, through His body.

Chapter 17

Life on the Hill

A week had gone by. I called Arlin. I finally gathered the courage to share with him what I had been through, what I was learning about myself, and for what I needed to apologize.

He wanted no part of anything I had to say.

Arlin was giving me the, "You just need to forget about me; run to God and let Him love you," scenario. Oh come on. Now he was patronizing me. He went from fiancé to self-appointed counselor. The only glimmer of hope he gave me was the suggestion for me to maybe come down to Pennsylvania and move into an apartment and then we could possibly date and see how things progressed. From engaged to possibly dating? I was devastated, distraught and becoming doubtful.

I began believing the enemy's lies because I had let go of the vision. I had spoken to Pastor Tim after church on Sunday relaying to him all the recent events, the most recent episode being a phone call from Arlin's mother. She read Scripture over the phone that spoke about the tongue. She asked me how I could be a Christian and say some of the things I was rumored to have said. It had gotten back to the family—remember that information highway?—that another member of the family overheard me curse in a fit of anger. One who used such language obviously could not qualify to be a Christian. The sad part was that Arlin's mom had an incredible gift of encouragement. She always believed the best about everyone and gave everyone the benefit of the doubt; she too, however, was also receiving extreme pressure to side with the rest of the family. Up until this point, she had been standing alone with Arlin. But now she joined the others in their stand against me.

Tim agreed to call Arlin from New York City on Monday. Tim told me he thought he would be able to determine in minutes where Arlin was coming from. But Tim shared with me he was not as concerned with Arlin's hesitations as much he was concerned with the phone call from Arlin's mom. He wanted to know if they had the real Gospel, or were they— meaning Arlin, too— under a doctrine of works. If that were the case, then Arlin would not be a suitable husband for marriage. I began to give this some thought.

The environment Arlin was raised in is a very homogenous community. Everything on the outside looks so lovely, but nobody really knows what's going on behind closed doors. This was quite different than my family culture, where everything was out in the open, for all to see and hear. Of course, there are Christian moral absolutes and standards of behavior that we are all called to walk in, to aspire to achieve through the work of the Holy Spirit and the grace of God in our lives. But, my experience with this community so far had been one of silent rejection or, better said, passive aggression. With the exception of the more outspoken ones, you had no idea what they were thinking.

The judgment is there, though, behind those closed doors. It might appear as though you are being let in, or "tolerated," while the reality is you are being rejected collectively by the group. You are not one of the community; you are an outsider. As a result, you feel the way only an outcast can feel. I was definitely a foreigner to them.

The same morning I spoke with Tim, mom called from Texas and we prayed. She tried desperately to encourage me, to calm me down and reassure me that Arlin would overcome his doubts. While we were praying, I had a vision of Mary, the mother of God. The Lord reminded me through that vision what she had to endure to birth the Christ. She had to face community rejection over an immaculate conception, a teen pregnancy and if that wasn t enough, a fiancé who left her for fear of losing his own reputation! The angel of the Lord had to convince Joseph that what seemed to be a dilemma was truly of God that Mary wasn t lying! On the last point, I could relate. I felt the Lord saying, "If you're willing to humble yourself and take the blame, I'll birth the real Christ in these people." I didn't know what He meant at the time. I just acknowledged it and went on.

Tim called me after he got off the phone with Arlin. He said, "Deborah, he's not ready to 'can' the relationship, but he's been shaken. I understand because I'm from Pennsylvania and my wife, Kathy, is Italian, like you. In Pennsylvania, if the glass is half full, they'll say it's a quarter full, where as you and Kathy would say the same glass was three quarters full. They exaggerate to the other extreme in an effort to seem humble. It's their culture and it's yours to make everything big and exciting.

"Let me give you an example," he went on to say. "Kathy and I went to a car dealer the other day because we needed a car. She told the salesman we had to have a car immediately! Well, we don't have to have one *immediately*, but within the next several months. Yes, I corrected her, but I understood. I would have said, 'We're just looking.' That's the difference."

He suggested that I do whatever Arlin asked me to do in terms of continuing our relationship. "But, Tim," I said, "he wants me to move back to Pennsylvania, get some crummy little apartment, and work locally in some ridiculous job so we can get to know each other better with no guarantees that we'll even date! No way! I'm not going back down there to that place and leave my friends, my church—basically my life—for a *maybe!*

"Deborah, if that's what he needs you to do, do it. If Jesus could go to the cross for you, what's six months?" Tim said.

Unfortunately, where else did I have to go? If Jesus would lead me back to Pennsylvania, I would have to follow, even if it meant putting aside my pride and feelings of resentment.

Arlin called that night and said he needed my parents' phone number in Texas to officially call off the wedding. I gave him the number. He called and spoke to my father. Until this day, neither of them will tell me exactly what occurred during that conversation or what was discussed specifically. All I knew was that Arlin had called my folks about 10 p.m. that night. At 1 a.m., he called me to say, after speaking to my father, he realized he had made a *big* mistake.

I wanted to know what happened that caused Arlin to call me back with a completely different tone in his voice. What did they talk about for almost two hours? What I gleaned from the questions I asked was that my father had given him a huge lecture about unconditional love. He had said something to the effect of: "So what if she exaggerates! Is she a murderer? Does she rob banks? Is she a liar?"

My dad, having grown up in New York City during the Great Depression, when Italians were called "dagos," low class, and were mocked and made fun of, had a deep sense of compassion and mercy for what I had just been through with this Mennonite family and their community. Arlin had grown up in a strong religious German community, somewhat devoid of outward or demonstrative emotional expression.

There is a certain charm, naiveté, and sense of security when growing up in a homogenous community without television and other 'worldly' things. But it s to the exclusion of others and their cultural realities. I had to keep all this in mind so as not to blame Arlin for this. I realized I had been judging him the same way he was judging me. We both had to realize that we are different. If our relationship was going to work at all, it would be through

God molding us and growing us, together. This thought gave meaning to the scripture about 'iron sharpening iron.'

Arlin's voice was warm but determined when he called me back that night. We both apologized and I could feel us melting together, even over the phone line. He said, "Come to Lancaster. I want you to catch the next train out." Without hesitation I said, "Ok."

The next train out was at 6:30 a.m. He called to wake me at 4:30 a.m. so I could dress and arrive at Penn Station on time. I boarded the train taking only the clothes on my back and my purse. It reminded me of when I first left for Pennsylvania and I felt the Lord saying, "Only take one cloak".

The three hour train ride seemed like an eternity. When the train finally pulled into the station, it was like a scene from the movie *Love Story*. It was a cold, dreary, November day. And when I looked out the passenger car window, there was Arlin sitting on the platform bench, alone in the lightly falling rain. He stood as the train rolled to a stop. He held a dozen long-stem red roses in his hands. He looked weary, expectant, and in love all at the same time!

I stepped down off the train with caution. I wasn't sure what to expect. Arlin ran to meet me, roses in hand. He grabbed me and hugged me so tightly without saying a word! I couldn't help myself, I kept saying, "I love you," over and over again. I felt so safe in his warm embrace. We left the train station, his arm around me, holding me. I kept wondering what he was thinking. His smile was relaxed and real, but he still had not said anything.

We went for coffee. He kept staring at me across the table. I didn't know what to make of it or what to say. Finally, he said, "Let's go back to my place." The 25-minute drive to his home was in total silence. Neither one of us said a word. We walked into his home and I looked around in disbelief. It looked like a hurricane hit it. Before we could even sit down he said, "I have to go down to the farm. I'll be back shortly." He headed for the door.

The Holy Spirit nudged me and before I knew it, I was making the offer, "Do you want me to clean this up for you?" My inner monologue was—*are You kidding? After he just called off our wedding and what he put me through, You want me to clean his house?! Forget that love-your-enemy line. Do I look like Merry Maids, here? And I have on my good black velvet dress!* But, I can't fight city hall…or God for that matter. Arlin smiled a tired smile and nodded, yes. He then walked out. I sighed heavily and began to clean. I was still in my good dress; I had brought nothing to change into.

As I was cleaning, I wondered if this was all there was, sounding much like that Peggy Lee song! *God, do You want me to move here, marry this man, live in this trailer on the top of a hill, and never be heard from again for the rest of my life? Just do laundry, cook, clean, and be his wife? That can't be my destiny. I'll just die, God!* Then I fell to the floor and began to sob deeply.

Then a thought occurred to me. Maybe I was supposed to end it face to face and that's why I was here. Maybe I *never* heard from God and I was incredibly deceived by my own desires! Inner conflict set in and I could feel the anxiety reaching a fever pitch in my head. My face felt flush. Suddenly, my nose began to bleed profusely, dripping all over his carpet. Oh no, not this, too? I get nose bleeds whenever I get extremely upset or desperately emotional.

Frantically, I began to clean his carpet. As I scrubbed, I only made a bigger mess. Fortunately for me, the carpet was dark brown and orange shag, the 1970's look. As soon as the relief of that thought washed over me, a more anguishing thought followed: cleaning ugly, brown and orange, 1970's carpet was to become my destiny! I started to bawl anew.

I finished cleaning up the mess and continued to clean the rest of his place. I figured I would prepare dinner for him, and then take the evening train back to the city. I would just call the whole thing quits, chalk it up to deception, and start my life over in New York City. I was now operating in reality mode. I had finally seen the light. I would never fit in here and I would never be accepted as one of them.

With new resolve, I went out to buy groceries for dinner. No reason why I shouldn't leave things on a positive note. A good meal and a "good-bye" seemed very fitting. Upon returning to his place, I found that he was already home. I began cooking, but I knew I had to break the news to him that this just wasn't going to work for me. What had been running through my head the whole time was my father's only reservation he had voiced during this courtship. He had warned me to be careful that I didn't let these people try to change me. He wanted me to be free to be me, to continue to pursue my dreams and aspirations. He believed in me.

"I have something to tell you," I said.

He sat down at the kitchen table. "I have something to tell you too," he replied. "You go first."

"No," I said, "you say what you have to say first."

"Well," he said, "I just came back from talking to my parents. I told them I didn't care what they said, I didn't want to marry someone I can live with, I want to marry someone I can't live *without*. I told them that I can't live without you—and no matter what they say; I'm going to marry you. Deborah, I don't care what they think. Whatever you want me to do, I'll do it. I'm ready to sell the farm tomorrow! We can live in New York City. We'll sell this place and move. I'll get a job and you can do whatever you want. I don't care. All I know is that I don't want to—no, I can't be without you!"

I couldn't breathe. It was my turn to sit down. As I slid into a chair across from him at the kitchen table, I inwardly rolled my eyes at God, *'Are you kidding me? What next, Armageddon?'* Outwardly, I smiled and reached for his hands. As we looked into each other's eyes, he asked, "What did you want to tell me?'

I said, "Never mind" and melted in his embrace.

Chapter 18

The Wedding

Arlin had worked on the farm all his life. Basically, not much of a childhood—no summer camps, no lessons, no school sports. He just worked on the farm every day of his life from the time he was old enough to reach the pedal on the tractor, which was around the age of five. As he reached school age, he would get up at 4 a.m. to do the barn work, go to school, come home, more farm work, eat dinner, and go to bed. The next day, he would start the grueling routine all over again. He finally got his first afternoon off when he was 14 years old. He remembers having those three hours off and being elated!

This all seemed almost abusive, but over time, I learned this was pretty standard for most kids living in Lancaster County who were born to farming families. They couldn't afford to hire help, which meant the children became the laborers; very different from most American families, where a kid's biggest dilemma is, "Who will I play with today or what toy should I play with?

Arlin's family was particularly frugal. He and his siblings grew up without heat and his parents rented out rooms to tourists to help support the family. Farming wasn't—and still isn't—a "get rich" occupation. Until he was 21, he worked for his father for room and board. His mom, being the softie she is, would slip him spending money when he had the time to go out with his friends. He clearly didn't go out much and saved every penny; at 25, he bought the business from his father.

I knew in my heart it would be wrong to pull him away from everything he had worked for all his life. And I knew he had some unresolved family issues that would follow us no matter where we lived. These needed to be addressed before we could move forward and make any drastic changes in his life. Besides all this, God had clearly given him a gift for farming. So one day when we were talking about the future, I said, "Let's stay here. This is where

God has us and this is where we belong." He looked at me, incredulously, "Really?" he half laughed. I nodded.

After we both recovered from the shock of that revelation, we just held each other.

For the next ten days, we "hid out" at his place. We were like recluses on the hill. We were so happy! We didn't care *what* the neighbors said. This wasn't the most prudent thing we could have done, but it was our only refuge at the time. We had just given his family and friends a huge morsel of gossip to pass around. Not a wise move. We were fueling the fire...

Saturday, November 11, 1995

Genesis 37–44 Joseph's brothers hated him. They were jealous of his father's favor over him. "We shall see what shall become of your dreams!"

My journal read:
Deborah, here's what I want you to see in Joseph's story:
I work through ordinary events to bring dreams to pass, to do awesome things.
I work in narrow places.
I work through the fullness of time.

Look for those ordinary, narrow places in your life and give me the timing.

Arlin called my parents to ask their forgiveness and tell them the wedding was on again. For my mother, the big wedding was off. It was too late. She had already consulted her Emily Post book on wedding cancellations and had ordered the announcements stating the wedding was off. We tried to convince her to not send them, but she was unrelenting. She was still hurt and mad at Arlin, and I think a little worried we would change our minds again. It was her safety net to bow out of the drama. She told us to elope, do whatever we wanted to; she didn't care. She was not putting on a big wedding anymore.

Originally, Arlin had *wanted* to elope. He said he had been through the big "shebang" before and it was all for show. He wanted it to be intimate—only the two of us, the witnesses, and the minister. Deep down, I believe he knew what he would be in for if he announced to his family that he was getting married again. Months ago, when he proposed this idea, I told him I couldn't possibly marry without my parents' approval and presence. I had always trusted their wisdom and guidance and couldn't see being without them on the most important day of my life. Maybe I should have listened to him and done things his way. Things certainly couldn't have been worse, as far as my parents were concerned. They were still trying to make sense of it all. At this point, I wanted to wait until they cooled down and forgave Arlin. But would that happen? I wasn't sure, so I just kept praying.

In the meantime, Arlin and I began premarital counseling in preparation for our wedding, whenever that would be. We were referred by Arlin's pastor to a couple who was from outside of the community. The associate pastor and musical director, John, and his wife, Barbara were from Colorado. We loved their music ministry. Coming from outside the community, they had no problem accepting me or our marriage. However, John kept asking me during our sessions, "Deborah, just what do you plan to do when you move here?"

I was still thinking that my life wouldn't change much, just my marital status. I would be married versus single, with my aspirations and goals in tact. After all, that's what happened to *my* married friends. No change. Their lives continued as usual, only now they had to adjust to married life. Had I disengaged my brain at some point?!

John had asked us to list separately the things we liked about each other and then to share them with one another. I had listed thirty-six things I liked about Arlin. He listed six he liked about me. That should have been another clue to me about how most of our future conversations would go—I would outspeak him by a ratio of six to one!

It was time to reveal the items on each other's list. He read me his list first. The six things he liked about me were: loves the Lord, dreams big, intelligent, slave to God's will, attractive, and disciplined. And in keeping with the 6 to 1 ratio, I had thirty six! I didn't have the nerve to share mine. I skirted that list very carefully. I mentioned the top ten and left it at that. John then said, "Great. I can see that you are compatible, but Deborah, *what are you going to do after you get married and move here?*" I looked at him, my mouth gaping, having no clue as to what he was referring. Of course my life would continue as usual, only now it would be in Mt. Joy instead of New York. Again, what was it that I was not getting at this point—life in New York versus life in Mt. Joy—what did I think I was going to do? Truth is, I hadn't given it any thought at all; I was blinded by true love and never considered what came with the package.

During the ten days that Arlin and I were hiding out in our hill retreat, his family had summoned the "Benner Inquisition." They called a family meeting with the entire brood to inquire about my intentions. I didn't want to go to this meeting, but I remembered what God had shown me in the vision that day my mother and I prayed together by phone between Texas and New York.

I knew I had to go to the family meeting and ask forgiveness for whatever they had accused me of *and* take the blame. Then God would work mightily. But *nothing* in me wanted to do this. I did, however, agree to go.

Arlin and I met with John earlier in the day to pray about the meeting. We wanted wisdom and covering for what was about to happen. And, I was just plain nervous! I didn't totally understand what God was requiring of me at that point. And a facedown with the whole clan at once?! I was flat out scared.

That night at the farm, they were all sitting at one long table waiting for us. We arrived and were directed to two chairs in the middle of the clan. I brought along a yellow legal pad with a list of everything they had accused me of…from being worldly all the way to being arrogant and making up stories.

When I had finished reading the list out loud, I said, "Now, have I missed anything? Is there anything else I have been, done or said that has offended you that is not on the list?" They all shook their heads no.

One brother started to leave saying, "That's all I needed to hear and now I'm okay with you two getting married."

They were all ready to get up when the Italian rose up within me and I conquered my momentary fears and said, "Wait a minute! You have all stated what you dislike about me, declared all your complaints and offenses, now it's time you hear from *me* and about the way **I** feel." Their jaws collectively dropped; they weren't expecting that.

They remained seated. "For a family who holds themselves up to being so godly and has judged me for *not* being so; let me address your behavior toward *me*, someone you haven't even taken the time to get to know. I have known your son and brother for two and a half months now; I live next door to your oldest son and his wife; I live four miles from this farm and two miles from another brother—and *no one,* not *one* person from this family has ever come over to meet me. You've not even bothered to say hello, how are you, let's get to know each other, let's have coffee or tea or lunch, or anything. You have extended *nothing!*

My family lives over 1000 miles away, and my parents have been on the phone with Arlin nearly *every* day, talking with him and getting to know him. None of you women, with the exception of one, came to my bridal shower that the theatre gave me. When my mother came and sat down with you and asked if there were any questions, concerns or problems about her daughter marrying your son, you said there were none. And, yet, you have gossiped and whispered behind my back to the entire county. You have maliciously disgraced me with your tongues, yet you have the nerve to sit here and judge m*e!* You accused me of not being a believer because you heard that I had lost my temper, raised my voice and cursed.

Welcome to the real world among the living! How dare you be such an affront to me and to my family and sit here so smugly and judge us! And love? You're doing this out of love for your son and brother? Did you ever think to love him enough to give him the benefit of the doubt? Maybe Arlin has been praying and being led by God and for once in his life, not acquiescing to you!"

I calmed myself and then quietly continued, "I am very deeply offended by your behavior toward me and my family. You know *nothing* about me or who I am as a person. I'm guessing you still don't even know my last name because none of you have ever asked! It's Caldarola, by the way. I am Deborah Caldarola from New York City. I'm in love with your son and I'm going to marry him, with or without your blessing. But for Arlin's sake and if we are going to have any kind of future relationship, I think it should be *with!*"

Well…the room got very quiet. Finally, the oldest daughter said, "You know what? She's right. We have a problem in this family of telling everyone else what we think of a person instead of going directly to that person. We also avoid confrontation, and we gossip instead of dealing with things head on. She's right and we have been wrong. Deborah, will you forgive me for gossiping about you and talking behind your back?" Then something amazing happened. They all began to look at each other and then back at me. One by one, all around the table, each one of them asked me to forgive them. At the end, Arlin's mother asked that we all get in a circle and hold hands and pray. They each came up to me, gave me a hug, and welcomed me into the family.

I wasn't sure *what* had just taken place. All I knew was God's ways are not our ways and He had just moved on my behalf. Was this what He had meant by the vision I had while praying with my mom? If not, I couldn't imagine any future blessing greater than this one. But for now, this one would do just fine. How awesome is my God!

Wednesday, November 15, 1995

Father, tonight Arlin and I went over to have dessert with his family, and yet the real purpose was to reconcile with the family over our relationship. It was so beyond words for me that I'm not sure what to say. I'm still in awe of Your power and Your move in my life and in my heart—and now in the hearts of this family. It really does blow me away…

That was my simple journal entry the night of the amazing transformation I experienced and the acceptance I felt into Arlin's family. Even though I felt like I was beginning to make my way in the Lancaster community and growing in my understanding of the Mennonite culture, new doubts set in; I was beginning to lose my sense of self. I knew God brought Arlin and me together and it seemed that staying and working the farm was God's direction for us. But what was my part in it all? What would be my contribution? Did God still have a purpose for my acting talents, or was that just for a season?

Also, I was still unsure of our immediate future. Our wedding was officially cancelled; what next? We knew we were to be married, but where, when and how was it all going to come together, especially now that my mom had closed the door permanently on any formal kind of affair? Maybe the office of the justice of the peace was to be the setting of our nuptials, after all. Oh, the irony! In early December I lamented in my journal:

December 3, 1995

Who despises the day of small things? For whoever touches you touches the apple of his eye.... I will live among you and you will know that the Lord Almighty has sent me to you.... Be still before the Lord, all mankind, because He has roused himself from his holy dwelling!" (Zechariah 4:10; 2:8, 11, 13)

Father, I have not been operating from faith. I have been scared about my future and what to do about acting, etc. I don't understand yet why my wedding was cancelled, so all I can ask is, "What do You want to say to me and how do You want to change me?" I know You desire that I honor my mother, so help us. Lord, You know what to do and how to do it. So, please help us. Help me to plan or put together my wedding in New York and to have the other reception in San Antonio. Lord, only You can plan all this—and in the middle of Arlin's planting time. Please, Father, put it all together for us.

I decide to put my life in Your hands now and think not to my own needs, wants, and desires. You have placed me here to support this man and to love him and I'm not sure how, right now. Please help me to put his needs first. I need Your help to give You everything. It's so hard. I'm not sure how to balance it all. Please help me. I want to help him with all of his business. Please give us both wisdom and knowledge. And help me to be selfless. I try so hard, but my rebellious nature will not give in.

I struggled with my future and purpose, but I also was saddened by my parents' absence in my life. After the grand wedding party was called off, mom shut down. She wasn't interested in how things were going or what we were deciding. I knew she was still upset with Arlin for breaking off the engagement, but now I felt like she was cutting me off as well. Arlin sent a letter of apology to my mother. He also sent flowers, and he called, too, but no response. She refused his phone calls. As far as she was concerned, if I married him, that was my business; she was done with it all.

Arlin wanted to get married, no matter what, and he didn't want to wait any longer in case I changed my mind. He was sensing that I was becoming weak in this whole struggle with my parents no longer on board, and mentally I was preparing to return to New York. I had been making calls to former temporary agencies as well as my acting agencies trying to line things up for my return.

Several times he had made plans for us to go to the justice of the peace locally to get married. Each time, I backed down the day before we were to go. I simply could not get married without my parents and my family present. The doubts were increasing as the days were passing.

I continued to have doubts no matter how hard I tried not to. Things were just not going the way I had planned, the way I had dreamed. I went to my journals. I had to go back and read what God had spoken previously. I remembered an entry from some years earlier when He woke me up early one spring morning to speak to me about a husband…

Tuesday, April 13, 1993, 3:30 a.m.

Read 1 Timothy 2 and 3. A word from the Lord: "Remember the way of the Lord. You will have your covering of a husband. Let Me mold him and shape him and prepare him. He requires love and truth, patience and prayer. I am in the making process with him. He does not understand. You must pray for him that he will bend and submit to my hand, that he will repent and humble himself to My working in his life. You will see shortly in the days ahead a great change in this man. You will see his heart turn toward you in a way only I could have changed. You will see the power of My hand in a man. Do not be afraid of his background or financial situation—because your life is one of faith and prayer. He will know his purpose and be given strength and determination to walk this out. You cannot understand My ways, but must walk in trust. Continue to seek Me and ask of Me to fill your heart with My Son Jesus, to know Him as your friend, to walk by His side. Your husband is Your Maker. Your earthly husband is only a temporary covering. His choosing is only for now, but I have chosen you eternally. Go now. Pray and fast and see how I move mightily in these three days. You have been granted the grace to walk in a fast, to pray and seek my face. You will not have to scatter about seeking work. I will lower your rent and move you when I am ready. Your dwelling place is temporary and only a base from which to move you out. Your husband will not always travel with you, but will be your covering in prayer. He will be a man of prayer, deep devotion, and compliance to Me. Only I can create such a heart of intercession. You must learn humility. You have only to wait for me, on Me, as I go about lining up your path. Days are coming, days are here. You will not have to look for work, for your doors are being prepared. You must be prepared in prayer and fasting for when I move you. Your husband is a man of many sorrows, a very broken and bitter man. He is not submitted to My teaching or My hand in his life. He is now at the hour of My molding in his life and needs to be uplifted in prayer. He will not believe what I am about to do in his heart and life and you cannot second guess. It will be beyond all you could hope or imagine and I want to demonstrate to you the power of My hand in a heart so you will be able to walk in faith, hope, and trust—and show the nations My power to deliver and save. I must take the broken and contrite, the lowly and the foolish to confound the wise of this earth, even my own children—as My children often interpret My ways and My moving, which they cannot do, but try in their hearts to reach My understanding. Trust is the word for the hour and you, My darling, must lean on Me for this trust. Continue to seek Me and ask, as I will pour out to you in abundance. Days are coming; days are coming; prepare ye the way of the Lord. Prepare ye the way of the Lord. Make room in your heart for Me. Open your heart, your soul, and your mind to Me."

What shocked me about this particular entry was that it came at the same time Arlin's former wife was leaving and divorcing him for another man. It was also when Arlin first experienced God and became a believer. I was actually praying for him and his salvation and didn't even know it! He was truly that "broken, contrite and seeking man," the one who would become my husband three years later! My resolve returned.

One afternoon I was flipping through the calendar, and I mentioned to Arlin it was going to be my mother's birthday on December 12. Without telling me, he decided to overnight her fresh peas and corn he had just harvested that fall. He packed them in dry ice and Fed-Exed them to Texas. That broke the "ice" for my mom. I couldn't believe it, peas and corn?!

Mother called to thank Arlin. In this simple phone call, she forgave him. Then, she surprised us further; she told us my family would be at their home December 23 to celebrate Christmas early with the ten grandchildren. She and Dad were leaving for Aruba on the 24th. She suggested the 23rd would be a good time for us to get married! She further explained that because all the family would be together it would be a perfect time for the family to welcome Arlin and to have a celebration of our marriage, "Nothing fancy," she added quickly, just to make sure that there would be nothing to cancel, if anything, God forbid, went south. She had to get my father's approval, however, and promised she would call back once she spoke to him.

Five days went by and I was in quiet anguish. Either I was getting married in two weeks with my parents' blessing or I was back in the land of the unknown, with no future plans and no clue as to the next step. Finally, she called back on the 17th with a yes! By this time, Arlin had moved down to the farm so that his family and neighbors would calm down. We were quite the talk of the town, now that we had been cohabitating for several days!

They all soon realized that our relationship was real and we were getting married no matter what. We called the airlines on the 18th and booked our flight, but a huge snowstorm was on its way. All the flights were being cancelled. We managed, however, to board the last flight on the 20th.

We arrived in Texas on Wednesday, the 20th, at almost midnight. The next two days were a blur, with a flurry of activity. I went from planning a grandiose affair with multiple bridesmaids to a living room gathering with family. But so many things still had to be taken care of: get the marriage license, ask the pastor to preside, order a cake and cater the food. We basically wrapped up all the details of a simple but beautiful wedding in 48 hours. We even went to our family jeweler to borrow a ring for Arlin until one could be made and shipped to him.

I know I should have been excited and walking on air as I floated around with the love of my life next to me as we prepared and planned what would be one of the most important days of our lives. But the truth is, I cried most of those two days because it was not the way I had envisioned things. I had dreamed, all my life, of walking down the long aisle of a beautiful ornate, Gothic cathedral where my father would escort me into the arms of my adoring husband-to-be. I could almost hear the majestic tones of the organ playing *something* in B minor. (Okay, allow me a little drama!). But now there was no aisle, no church, no friends, and no organ playing in the background. It was a simple ceremony with just family; my sister's neighbor took pictures. The only thing even remotely "foo-foo" were my mom's poodles. Thank God for the poodles, they classed up the place!

At the last minute, my mom did 'allow' two of my friends to attend. One was a girlfriend, Carrie, who brought along her guitar to give us some accompaniment of music and song. With no time to coordinate with the pastor, he didn't take his cues for the interjection of songs. He cut her off in the middle of her playing and singing a few times. Par for the course! My other friend who attended was Don, a dear friend, who had become like a brother to me over the past ten years.

The ceremony went okay. Wearing my beautiful wedding dress, I took my father's arm and came down the staircase; at least I had that much. Dad cried (so, I did get a little drama after all!!!). No one from Arlin's family was present. His mom sent roses, which ended up in a few of the photos. That was the extent of his family's presence.

After the ceremony, we sat down for Christmas dinner and wedding cake. Following the meal, the entire family got up and moved into the family room to open their Christmas gifts.

I looked around, and there we were—Arlin and I—sitting at a beautiful table with a half-eaten wedding cake— *alone*. Not quite the wedding reception of my dreams. Some might have said it was cozy. And really, it was. But at the time, I kept fighting the thought, *is this it?*

Shortly after, my siblings left with their children and their gifts. The poodles stayed. Arlin and I were *still* sitting alone at this huge table, me in my wedding dress and he in one of my father's tuxedos. Mom came out of her bedroom, which was just off the family room, in her housecoat, and that's when I knew the evening was over.

I was feeling very sad at this point. It was if our wedding was just another thing on the list of events for the evening; eat dinner, open presents, have dessert, watch Arlin and Deborah make a lifelong commitment…wait, what was that last one? As far as the grandchildren were concerned, the gift-opening part totally upstaged the rest of the evening's program.

Arlin and I gathered up our things and got ready to go to our hotel. My parents had arranged for us to have two nights in a lovely suite downtown on the river.

As we left, no one was waiting outside the house to throw rice or send us off. We just got in the car alone, no fanfare, no waving crowd, and drove to the hotel. I pouted, just a little, the whole way. However, God is so kind. He knew our desires; especially mine. When we arrived at the hotel downtown, it became apparent that a professional basketball team was staying there, as well. Fans had gathered to wait for the team to return from the Alamo Dome.

When we pulled up to the portico to drop off our car, the basketball fans saw us get out of the car, me in my wedding dress and Arlin in his tux. More than 100 onlookers cheered and clapped. That was an amazing, unexpected surprise! Not exactly rice or rose petals, but they celebrated our union and made our night, even if they didn't know who we were!

When I say that the cheering of perfect strangers was the highlight of our night, I wasn't exaggerating. The sex certainly wasn't. I'd like to say that our wedding night was this Star-Spangled Banner kind of experience with fireworks and dazzling lights popping off everywhere. But the truth is, and I'm sure to Arlin's disappointment, it was not. I was still reeling over being left at the dinner table by my family for the opening of Christmas presents, the absence of my extended family, my Godparents, and my closest friends (all 200 of them). Ok, now that's a funny exaggeration. I have only about fifty closest friends, the rest are friends, distant friends and acquaintances, for the record. But in any event, since I had cried all day because I wasn't being walked down the aisle of a beautiful cathedral, I was exhausted.

The morning of our ceremony I wouldn't even get out of bed. My exasperated mom sat on the edge of my bed interrogating me about what she could do to redeem the situation. "What, what do you want? Do you want candelabras, flowers, streamers, what? Tell me what I can do to make it better," her New York accent was notched up, full volume in her understandable frustration.

My cranky attitude and wedding disappointments seem kind of ridiculous, looking back, now. Just a reminder to women… it's the man remember? Not the wedding location or the perfect celebration, it's the man, it's about the marriage, not the wedding! I had forgotten.

If I had to do it over again, first and foremost, I would have trusted Arlin, gone to the Justice of the Peace and tied the knot the week after we got engaged— as he pleaded with me to do. I could have had the party later. It would have saved a lot of grief, time, and money. He knew what was coming when he announced he was engaged; I did not. Lesson learned.

Secondly, even though my dream wedding was cancelled, my wedding *night* was not. If I could do it all over, that would have been completely different, too. I would have (literally) embraced this incredible man God had given me, celebrated what He had put together, and realized that I'd entered into a union, by God's grace, which no man could separate. After all, it truly was the beginning of the rest of my life with this wonderful man and our journey had just begun. Instead, I was pouty.

For the record, pouty sex is not sexy -- for anyone, Arlin included. If I had realized this then, perhaps right now, you would be reading a steamy section of this book that certainly would have had to be edited out!

Eventually, I did get over myself and the steam began to rise…and still does. I'll leave it at that.

The next two days at the hotel really were quite magical. It was Christmastime, so the lights and decorations along the river were gorgeous. We relaxed and tried to take in the magnitude of what had just taken place during the previous week: a yes from mom, a flight to Texas, and a wedding— *our* wedding. Wow!

After our hotel stay, we went back to my parents' home for the next ten days. We had agreed to house-sit for them while they vacationed in Aruba. Our first Christmas and New Year's together was spent in Texas. The original honeymoon—three weeks in South America, the Galapagos Islands, Argentina, and Peru—cancelled. We visited with family and friends instead.

At the end of our stay, we met Mom and Dad at the airport. They were arriving from Aruba as we were simultaneously departing for Pennsylvania and our future life together. We all sat in the airport restaurant for a bite to eat before our flight. We chatted about their holiday and our honeymoon. It was fun and a bit surreal to sit at a table across from my parents. Here I was in this freshly entered marital status sitting next to my new husband. I was part of a new 'club,' now: the married-for-lifers. We laughed and joked and I felt, somehow, older and wiser. We were like them, now. We were indeed… married folk.

Chapter 19

Culture Shock

Back in Pennsylvania, no family or friends waited for us at the airport when we arrived; there were no signs, no welcome-home parties, no acknowledgment of any kind. His dad picked us up at the airport, and the 20-mile ride back to the farm was *pretty* quiet.

Another major snowstorm moved in immediately after we returned. Due to the rapid snow accumulation, the milker, the farmhand scheduled for the night milking, couldn't reach the farm. That meant Arlin and I had to milk the cows! That was a first in my life—and my new *married* life at that! Sink or swim, as my mom always says…

I walked out of the trailer ready to milk cows. I was dressed in my Donna Karan snow boots, a designer sweater, and my black suede jacket. Arlin didn't tell me what to expect, nor did he take note of what I was wearing and that I was, to say the least, inappropriately dressed. We jumped on the snowmobile and off we went. Arlin was on automatic pilot regarding the cows; the milking was getting started late and those girls were waiting!

When we arrived at the barn, Arlin went immediately into the milking parlor and I followed right behind him. I watched as he systematically set things up, his hands maneuvering machinery and getting everything ready. Then he turned to me and said, "Ok, go get the cows up."

Do what? I stood there stunned, I didn't know what that meant, "get the cows up." He stayed busy but then turned to me and said, a little more forcefully this time, "Go ahead, go out into the barn and get the cows up!" Well, okay, then. I guess I'll go "get the cows up." I'll go out there and start telling those 1500 pound animals to come on up to the milking parlor. I didn't know what I was going to do exactly, but I was determined to try. I stepped into the barn and into three inches of cow manure, walking around gingerly, so as not to start a stampede, (or mess up my Donna Karans.) I began saying in a very shy voice, "Come on girls, get on up now, come on", tapping one or two lightly on the hind end to motivate them. The gals weren't budging.

Ten minutes later Arlin came out of the parlor shouting, "What are you doing?"

"Getting the cows up!" I screamed, louder than I had spoken to any of the girls! As he watched what I was doing he laughed and said, "No, no, no, you don't talk to them like that, you take this stick, bang it on the railings and yell, "Get up, let's get a move on! Come on up, girls!!" They responded to his voice immediately and started heading towards the holding area where they lined up and entered the milking parlor. He returned to the parlor and left me out there to finish the job; there were more girls to "encourage" into the parlor. Twenty minutes later, he returned, seeing that I hadn't finished the job, "What is going on?!"

There was this one cow that was all cozy in her bed and not going anywhere. I kept nudging her on the behind to get her up but she was not budging. He watched, suppressing a laugh and said, "Deborah, you have to get in front of her and bang on the neck railing with the stick to *make* her move." He did this and it worked for him. This girl was big! I didn't want a stampede, for Pete's sake. "Give me a chance here, Frankie Farmer!" I thought to myself.

I returned to the milking parlor, where things seemed to be going smoothly; I was freezing. As it turned out, my designer snow boots? Not waterproof. But there was this thing; it looked like a giant blow torch shooting out flames to keep the parlor warm and the milkers from freezing. It reminded me of a mini jet engine spewing fumes out the back end. I kept walking over to it and holding up my Donna Karans to warm up my frost bitten toes. The torch was melting those plastic boots; this was not going well at all. Arlin kept working, not paying any mind to me and my insignificant problems. Hello? Every extremity was turning purple. But he had his own issues; those girls had to be milked. As I shivered there, frozen to the core, I marveled at how much there was to know about this cow-milking process. I had new respect for this man I had married and new understanding of the farm life I had just stepped into.

We finished milking at about one o'clock in the morning and snow was still silently falling; accumulating all the while. The snowmobile couldn't make it back up our quarter-mile driveway to the trailer. The motorized skis just sank in the four feet of snow. So, at 1 a.m., after milking the cows in freezing cold weather, in my melted snow boots, we *trudged* up the hill. Arlin dragged me most of the way up the hill behind him as I whimpered along, completely sure I was going to lose my fingers and toes to frost bite. We got to the door of the trailer only to find that it was nearly blocked by a snow drift. Arlin had to lift me up and shove me over the snow to get me in the door; the snow was so deep I couldn't step over it to get in! We both fell to the floor, laughing. I looked up at the ceiling and I cried out, "Oh my God! What have I done?!?!?!"! Arlin just kept laughing and then leaned over to kiss me. *Welcome* to married life on the farm!

When we finally dropped into bed that night, I started giggling. Arlin asked me what was so funny. I reminded him that when I was performing in the Noah play, back in the fall, I was in one scene with a live cow, milking it and singing a song that went, "Milking the cow and feeding her hay is only a start!" Scary how prophetic *that* scene was! Doing the scene 12 times a week for 18 weeks was prepping me for what was to come. Milking the cow and feeding her hay *was* only a start!

Chapter 20

It's Official

For the first two months of our marriage—for that matter, the first two years—I was in culture shock. At the end of February, though, Arlin's mother held a drop-in reception for us. She invited his entire family (most of the community) and friends. I insisted on wearing my wedding dress; maybe to make a point or maybe just for fun. I was going to get mileage out of that dress one way or another!

This was the first time his family celebrated a second marriage. Some people went through the reception line and greeted me normally, while others refused to shake my hand or acknowledge me. I was trying to understand. I guess it really is different when you have been raised for generations in a small, closed-off community like this with all of their traditions, customs, and beliefs.

I made it through the event, despite those who refused to shake my hand or acknowledge me in the receiving line. It was funny, really. Here it was, *my* wedding celebration and some family members and friends declined to shake my hand? That's got to be a first in some book of records. Makes me wonder, why did they come?

After that evening, it was official. We were married and I wasn't going anywhere. Some accepted the marriage, others not, still others were not sure what to make of the "loud NYC actress turned farmer's wife."

I thought back to John's question, the music minister who kept asking me during our premarital counseling, "Deborah, what do you think you are going to do living here in rural America on a dairy farm?" I remember answering him, "I don't know, continue to travel back and forth to NYC, do auditions, book work and come home to the farm after a shoot." Sounded like a plan to me! Which is essentially what I did; I went to Philadelphia and signed with an agent there and traveled back and forth for auditions to NYC and Philly, occasionally booking a commercial or trade show. The traveling quickly got old, and I missed Arlin, so in addition, I took the Pennsylvania's teachers' exam to get licensed in PA so I could substitute teach. A Spanish teacher in Lancaster County was in high demand. I had constant work in that arena. And so it went – I traveled to NYC, Philly, and taught Spanish at the local high schools. I needed something to keep me busy. I had no close friends or family nearby, and Arlin worked practically 24/7 on the farm; he was glad I had things to do to keep me busy.

And, ever so slowly, I learned to love and appreciate the good here and to be thankful for all that God had done in our lives over the past year. I do have to confess though, sometimes, the whole thing felt somewhat like a dream. Did this really happen? Am I really the wife of a dairy farmer? Is this really my life… or just some crazy dream?

The story of Joseph in the Bible, the guy with the coat of many colors, continues to encompass my thinking. He had a wild dream and then was sold into slavery by his jealous brothers. Later, he was thrown into the dungeons of Egypt—*twice!* I'm sure he wasn't singing Disney's " Zippity Doo Dah" all along. He was pleading with the butcher, the baker, and the candlestick maker saying, "Remember me down here in this hole when you're set free and *get me out of here!"* And, in due season, God delivered Joseph and his dream did come to pass. Not the way he thought, of course, but nevertheless, God's purpose for his life came to light, and then his dream made sense. By the way, what happened to the butcher, the baker, and the candlestick maker? They forgot about Joseph. But God didn't. And He'll never forget about us, either, or the dreams he's given us. I'm convinced that some day we will all "wake-up" and by God's infinite grace, this life will all make sense.

PART TWO

THE CHILDREN

Your will be done.
(Matthew 6:10)

Chapter 21

July's Child

One morning, I woke up and eight years had gone by. It's funny how you long for, anticipate and pray for a time to come in your life; then when it does, you so quickly become accustomed to the "new normal" of your day to day living. It becomes difficult to imagine your life before or imagine it any other way. I can't say the time flew by, but it was a full-time occupation to navigate this new world: the life of a farmer's wife in a Mennonite community.

By this time, I was definitely a *little* more integrated into Arlin's family and in fact, had just returned from spending a week with my in-laws and extended family down at the Outer Banks; Nags Head, North Carolina, *without* Arlin. Arlin was unable to go because of the fall harvest. Right before I left, Arlin was having the worst week of farming he had ever experienced. Three weeks earlier, a hurricane came through and leveled all the corn. The cornfields, which normally had 12-foot stalks shooting straight up in the air, were now lying flat, like a bulldozer had run over them. The harvesters had a difficult time getting under the corn stalks, so the yield was down 30%. That's a lot of corn left in the fields. Arlin and all the farmers in the area had just experienced the roughest week of farming ever. Arlin had planned on joining me at the beach after the harvest, but it didn't happen.

I was a tad anxious about being on vacation with Arlin's five brothers and sisters, their spouses, children, *and* his parents, *alone*. But, I needed the break and it was free! I figured, if worse came to worse, I could just stay in my room and read. I drove down with Cheryl, one of my sisters-in-law. Of my four sisters in-law, she and I are probably the most alike in terms of temperaments so I felt the eight-hour drive with her wouldn't be too difficult.

Surprisingly, the whole week turned out to be extremely relaxing for me. Every morning, one of the brothers or brothers-in-law would do a family devotion after breakfast. I remember sitting on a double-sized chair, with two of my nieces sitting next to me while I painted their toes. I thought to myself, "This is *not* the family I experienced eight years ago when I first met Arlin." For the first time, I really felt like I *was* a family member, as opposed to just being *married* to one. We had all come a very long way.

Arlin and I had since walked through some unforeseen, excruciating heartbreaks and difficult changes, but also received some surprising blessings. Through each one, God brought us to our knees only to lift our heads to see His glory…and be changed. Let's start with the heartbreaks…

Before we were married, when we met with Pastor Tim in New York, the subject of children was addressed. I insisted we go on some method of birth control as soon as we were married because I wanted to wait at least four years before having children. "From the womb to the tomb" my mother always says. Once you have kids, you can't put them back! And all my friends with children echoed her by saying, "They change your life drastically and forever." Children are a huge blessing, just a time- and energy-consuming one!

My immediate goal had been time alone with Arlin. I reasoned we would need at least four years to get to know one another before adding children to the mix. I had it all worked out. Arlin, on the other hand, was not for family planning, at least not for us. He felt having children was in God's hands. Of course, we weren't starting out at age 20, which made his thinking a little easier to acknowledge. After all, we didn't have time to end up with 12 kids.

I argued for the alternative. I eventually wanted to have four or five kids; I just didn't want to start quite yet. I wanted time to adjust to married life and to one another.

Pastor Tim suggested waiting wasn't a bad idea, but definitely not any longer than two years. I'm sure he reasoned because of my age at the time Arlin and I married, we should start a family sooner rather than later. Tim's suggestion bought me the "valued" answer I was looking for: more time!

On our visit to Texas following our meeting with Tim, when Arlin was meeting my family for the first time, I went to my doctor to get the usual pre-marital blood work and testing done. I discussed the matter with him. Together we agreed on a family planning method that would be good for Arlin and me. I'm sure my doctor assumed Arlin was on board as well. Why not? I hadn't told him any differently. My plan was to wait until after the wedding to let Arlin in on the decision. He didn't need more to think about in the midst of everything else going on then. I was being…thoughtful.

Of course, I wasn't prepared the day of our wedding. That whole ordeal was such last-minute high drama, who had time to think about *family planning?* I was just trying to get married, for Pete's sake!

Well...I got pregnant...right off the bat! Never had the chance to put my well-intentioned plan into effect, be it as it were, without Arlin's consent. So much had happened that I hadn't taken much notice of my cycles. I skipped a couple without realizing it. It wasn't at the top of my list of concerns in the beginning. Surviving life on "the hill" was.

Standing at our kitchen sink one day, I remember turning to Arlin sitting at the table saying, "You know, come to think of it, I haven't had my period in a while. Oh well…" I thought it was probably because of all the stress and didn't pay any attention. Surprise!

I didn't tell anyone other than Arlin. After what we had just been through, how could I go through more rejection with his family? I had no illusions of anyone being excited for us—or should I say, for me? This would mean my permanence among them. I went about my business, as usual, without a word. Little did I know the fate that awaited this pregnancy.

It happened one night while we were milking. I doubled over in pain while in the milking parlor. Arlin rushed over to me and I told him I felt really sick. I was having excruciating pain in my lower abdomen. By now, I was about two months' pregnant. I still hadn't told anyone—not anyone locally, anyway.

Arlin carried me out to the truck and drove me up to the trailer. Then he carried me into the house and put me into bed. The milking wasn't finished and I knew if Arlin didn't return, the milk wouldn't go out on time which would cause a chain of repercussions, logistical as well as financial. I assured him I was better and insisted he go back down to the milking parlor. Reluctantly, he did. It was about 1 a.m.

Truthfully, I was scared and in pain. I didn't know what was happening to me. Desperate, I called my sister in Texas about two in the morning, my time. I explained to her what I was experiencing. I had enormous cramps, like my body was forced to contort and I rolled up in a ball, cringing with pain. Then I would have to run to the bathroom…and blood, lots of it, spilled out of me. When I asked her what was happening. She said, "Deb…you're miscarrying." I was in shock and still dealing with the immediate pain. It was an awful ordeal, emotionally and physically.

I remember looking out the window that night, between episodes to the bathroom, staring out at the full moon gleaming in the night sky. I was hurt and becoming angry as I stared out realizing that the creator of that moon and the entire universe, for that matter, was allowing me to lose this baby. How could He do such a thing? I felt the Holy Spirit gently say to me, "And who are you to say when life begins and ends?"

I closed my eyes, tears streaming down my cheeks, and I shuddered. In the quietness of my heart and through my agonizing tears, I was silenced. Silenced by an omnipotent God reminding me just who is in charge and in whose hands I rest my life. I made my way back to the bed for the last time. It was finally over.

I fell asleep thinking about His Word, "For my thoughts are not your thoughts, neither are your ways my ways," declares the Lord. "As the heavens are higher than the earth, so are my ways higher than your ways and my thoughts than your thoughts" (Isaiah 55:8–10).

Up until then, my erroneous thinking meant that I decided when I was ready to have kids, and then I'd have them. Oh sure, God is the one who gives life, but I'm the one who sets the time and place. After all, shouldn't God consult me about my schedule, my wants and desires… my time frame? Clearly not. It was another lesson to learn; more growing up to do. Hadn't I been through enough the last two years? I guess that was precisely the *antithesis* of His point.

I comforted myself emotionally by telling myself, "We've been married a relatively short time; therefore, we still have plenty of time to have children." Only now, I was on board with Arlin about 'family planning.' There would be none. That was God's business, not mine. End of subject.

After the loss, the desire for children seemed even more pressing. I was lonely in Mount Joy with neither close friends, nor immediate family. Arlin worked most of the time down at the farm. Sure, there was his family, but they still weren't as close as I would have liked. I dearly missed my friends in California, New York, and Texas. As a single person, I was able to be with my friends daily and travel and see those friends whenever I wanted. Here, I was pretty much stuck on the top of this hill, on this farm, away from civilization! "Okay, I got the husband and he's GREAT. Thank You, Jesus, but what about the rest of my life? And, what about a baby?"

Friday, August 23, 1996

Dear Father, I am disappointed I am not pregnant. Every time after I begin my cycle, I feel sad. Help me to trust You. You know when we will be ready to have children and You are the author of life. Lord, let Your will be done. But, if I could, I'd like to ask for twins—boys or girls, or one of each, perfectly healthy. Or just one. You know, Lord, what I can and cannot handle. I imagine with the farm right now, we can't afford children. But, Lord, You know. You are the author of our faith. Let Your will be done.

Two years after praying this prayer, I still hadn't conceived. Now I was beginning to have some doubts about my ability to get pregnant, again. Why was it taking so long, especially since we weren't doing anything to prevent it? The thought of not conceiving again had never entered my mind. I was positive God intended for us to have not only a family, but a big family. We both came from large families, seven kids in mine and six in his. Who was better equipped than us to have kids? We now lived in a rural community on a farm, possibly the best place to raise children. What more could one ask for?

Chapter 22

October's Child

Ash Wednesday, February 25, 1998

Lord, I'm so excited because I know I'm pregnant, and I believe You have shown me it's to be a little girl and we're to name her Abigail. Of course, I haven't had any tests yet, but I've missed a cycle and I can tell. If it's to be a boy or perhaps twins—well, You know what Your desire is for Arlin and me. He says he can't imagine being a father and holding a child. Is this Your timing? Lord, only You know.

All my doubts flew out the window when I tested positive for pregnancy again! I chose not to tell anyone this time for two reasons: fear of another miscarriage, and Arlin's youngest sister was getting married, and I didn't want to steal her moment. I figured we'd help her celebrate that family event and then, perhaps around Easter, I would announce our good news.

Mentally and emotionally I was traveling pretty fast through the next nine months of my life. I started planning, even though I was only at eight weeks. I was picking out colors and bedding—and thinking of themes for a nursery, a room that would continue to be the office, shared by the coming baby. Our trailer was small, but I could make it all fit and still look good. It was a matter of planning!

Something very strange and unusual happened, however, that until this day I can't explain. From that Ash Wednesday in February until April 2, I didn't once write about the pregnancy in my journal. I didn't pray about it in my journals; I didn't share my emotions, my expectations, my hopes, or my fears of losing this pregnancy. The journals were silent. Although I continued to journal regularly about other topics, I wasn't speaking to God about this child, not in writing anyway.

I thought the time to announce our good news would never come. I wanted to tell my parents first so we planned a trip to Texas to surprise my parents with a sonogram picture of the baby. By now, I was fourteen weeks and we had the champagne ready, so to speak.

Finally, it was time for our flight to Texas. We arrived that morning and I went straight to see my family gynecologist. I had scheduled a sonogram ahead of time in order to get a picture of the baby to show my folks that evening after the doctor's visit.

As the technician performed the sonogram, she grew very quiet. I wasn't thinking anything in particular; this was my first time having this done, so I didn't know what to expect. However, I began noticing a worried look across her face. She still hadn't said anything. Finally, she said, "Let me get the radiologist." I asked her what was wrong. She didn't answer or look back as she walked out of the room. I was left lying there on the table, alone, wondering what could possibly be the problem.

Moments later, she returned with the radiologist. Together they looked at the screen. I could see my beautiful baby. He or she looked about three inches in length on the screen. I didn't know what else to look for, or what were they looking for. But couldn't they see the tiny little perfect baby that I could see? What could possibly be wrong? Then the radiologist turned to me and placed her hand on my arm. "I'm so sorry, but we can't find a heartbeat," she said.

Arlin had intended to go with me for the sonogram, but we hadn't counted on my brother Vincent, a doctor in the same hospital, seeing us in the hallway. Vincent, upon seeing Arlin, gave him a big hug and invited him into his office to visit. Vincent was shocked to see us in Texas. We hadn't told anyone in the family we were coming. We wanted to surprise mom and dad first. When he asked what we were doing there in the office building, I quickly told the half-truth that I was in for my routine gynecology checkup. I still didn't have a regular doctor back in Pennsylvania. It would have given us away for Arlin to insist upon going with me, so we were kind of stuck. I smiled apologetically at Arlin as my brother led him down the hall in the opposite direction.

Arlin had been so excited to be with me for the first pictures of our baby, but I didn't want to give away our secret. Looking back, that was a grievous mistake. I received the heartbreaking news alone. I was totally unprepared. And how in the world was I going to break the news to Arlin?

After hearing "We can't find a heartbeat," I was in shock. I kept looking at the screen. *They have to be wrong, how could this be? I've carried this child for fourteen weeks and now there's no heartbeat?* I couldn't say anything; I just kept searching for any sign of even the slightest movement to prove them wrong. Surely they must be misreading something…but they weren't.

What was I to do now? I was too embarrassed to cry. Instead I said, "That's okay, thank you." The radiologist and technician kept apologizing. No one was there to comfort me; I could tell they felt at a loss of what to do or say next. All I wanted was to get off that table, get dressed, leave, and cry my guts out! I needed to get out of there fast; I could feel the dam about to break, and I wanted to be alone when it did.

I left the office and ran upstairs to my father's office. I had just started to cry, but I was still trying to control my emotions. I was afraid of what would happen if I just let go. I needed to tell Arlin the news as calmly as possible.

As I approached my father's door, he rushed out to meet me. The radiologist was a friend of his and had called him immediately to let my dad know what had happened. We were both crying as we embraced. "Why didn't you tell me you were pregnant?" he said.

"Because I wanted to surprise you, Dad," I sobbed. We held each other and wept together.

Then I went to find Arlin. He was in my brother's office. I ran up to him and hugged him, while crying hysterically. My brother had tears in his eyes. He didn't know I was pregnant, but from my reaction, he gathered I was there for a pregnancy test and it had come back negative.

"It's okay. You can get pregnant next month," he said, trying to reassure me.

"No," I muttered through hot tears, "You don't understand. I'm three and a half months pregnant now and they can't find a heartbeat!" There was silence in the room except for my muffled sobbing into Arlin's chest. Vince returned to his desk, put his head down, and began to cry. Arlin's arms went around me, I felt the warmth of his embrace and the weight of his pain as his breaths turned into quiet sobs. What else was there to do?

We went home and instead of a surprise dinner where we announced our good news, I went upstairs to bed. I wanted to go to sleep and escape the pain. That was, of course, impossible. This was loss number two, after a long wait for pregnancy as well as the expectation of sharing the good news with my family, who would have rejoiced with us with all their hearts. I was ready for this baby; I wanted this baby; I *needed* this baby! But alas, it was not meant to be.

However, God was ever so faithful during this dark hour. My mom and sister Jean were sitting at the kitchen table when Arlin and I arrived at the house. They were both in tears and had open arms for me. My father had placed a huge bouquet of wild flowers in a beautiful blue crystal vase on the wardrobe of our bedroom. The flowers were beautiful, something natural, to bring light and life to the room which seemed so sad, and so dark in my pain. And then there was the rest of my family. I couldn't thank God enough that this had happened to me while I was at home in Texas with my family.

Finally, we shared the news with Arlin's family back in Pennsylvania. I received a phone call from my sister–in–law Cheryl, who called to give her sympathy. Arlin received a call from his close friend, Lamar, encouraging him to keep believing. It was nice to have people from "home" to acknowledge our loss.

My doctor asked us to wait three days before taking any measures to confirm the sonogram results. I went back to the hospital on Monday, was given another sonogram, and then admitted for a dilation and curettage (D&C). Arlin stayed with me until I was wheeled into the Operating Room. My father was with me the whole time. It gave me comfort before I was given anesthesia to know he was there.

Clearly, I had a lot of questions for God during that time. I know that God hears all of our prayers and often gives clear answers. But often He asks for us to simply lean into Him and trust. At this juncture, the latter was the way it was for me. My prayers were ultimately unanswered in my quiet surrender. Strange how a time like this either draws you away from God or closer to Him. This time, it drew me closer as He poured out His love and grace to me before and after my return to Mount Joy. And even after this ordeal, I still had hope.

Chapter 23

R&R

Thursday, April 2, 1999
Lord God, Father, by the power of Your Holy Spirit, touch my heart today and heal me. Help me to trust You in surrender…to trust You even in the bad and perplexing times. While we were in Texas, we lost our baby. But, by Your grace, we're moving on. We must. You certainly blessed us with being in Texas so my family and friends could be there with me!

Christine and Emily are the names of my children in heaven. Thank You, Lord, for these children. Keep them safe and play with them until I get there…

Over the next year and a half, our business grew. Arlin had just asked me to give up acting and work full-time on the farm, which I did. After that, I didn't journal much about children or pray about conceiving again. I buried myself in my new role as 'farmhand' and was all but consumed with my daily to-do list, as Arlin felt more confident about my abilities and gave me more responsibilities.

From time to time, though, my thoughts drifted to the two little ones I had lost, wondering what they would have looked like, would I have been a good mommy…and then I'd snap back to the here and now, and re-focus on the present. There was always something that had to be done; a part to go pick up for a tractor or a cow that was calving. My thoughts and daydreams would have to wait.

I began to journal less and less, not only about the hope for a baby, but about everything else. Sometimes, I skipped a few days, an entire week, and eventually a month or two. When I did write during this time, I somehow omitted mentioning either my last two pregnancies or the losses. Journaling was my alone time with God, my time of prayer and reflection, but now I wasn't journaling at all. Slowly, I was drawing away from deep intimacy with God. The pain and the loss were too profound to discuss, even with Him. I put it all away.

That spring, Becky, my friend from New York, called and invited me to go to the Outer Banks of North Carolina. She had rented a beautiful ocean-front cottage for a month, and had asked me to join her. The whole idea of relaxing, reading books on the beach and taking a break from the farm was too good to be true. Arlin said he could spare me for a week or so and I was on the next train south.

With my old friend, I shared my losses and the emotional roller coaster I had been on. She was a great listener; full of compassion and mercy—and she made me laugh! We drank wine and told stories about our lives in New York. We laughed that whole first night.

The next morning, we headed out to the beach and I soaked up the sun and lost myself in books about other people's dramas; it was heaven. We took long walks, stopped for lattes, shopped the boardwalk, got bikini waxes, facials, haircuts, and rented what seemed like an *endless* number of movies. We must have rented every chick-flick available. We cried as each film ended, discussing plots, characters, and storylines. At night, we cooked and sipped wine while watching the beautiful colors of sunset on the ocean's waves. What a great time of healing this was for me; a time of forgetting and just having fun with someone who loves me and whom I trusted to share my pain.

Tuesday, May 18, 1999

Dear Father, Son, and Holy Spirit! Good morning and thank You for a wonderful week with Becky and her family at the beach. What a great, restful time it was for me, God! And, Lord, if it was the time for a planting of life in my womb—I receive Your child, Lord. I thank You and praise You for today!

I returned from my week at the beach with a sneaking suspicion that I might be pregnant again. And if that were true, I was sure that a restful week at the shore would have allowed me to secure a strong, healthy pregnancy. I had to wait until the end of the month to test, and when I tested, it was positive.

Friday, June 10, 1999

Father, Son, and Holy Spirit, how I have avoided You. I give You my fears about losing this child I carry. Help me to enjoy Your gift as long as I have this one. Help me to allow myself to rejoice. Deliver me of a negative spirit and give me a spirit of laughter and joy!

I was more cautious this time—trying to guard myself against getting too emotionally invested in this baby. But I couldn't help myself. I watched, waited, and counted each and every day, one by one. I prayed and hoped for one more day. If I could just make it past the fourteenth week, perhaps I would be home free and carry full term.

I found a good local doctor who had me go to the hospital for weekly blood tests to check my counts. They monitored me closely, checking my levels in case anything spiked or dropped below normal. I wasn't totally high-risk yet, but with two miscarriages behind me and the length of time it took me to conceive between pregnancies, I warranted close monitoring.

Week ten, the test results came back with low counts. The nurses told me I was losing the baby. I was having another miscarriage... my third. Again, I was alone when I received the news and this time, I was in Lancaster, Pennsylvania, not Texas. Although relations with Arlin's family had improved, being here wasn't the same as being with my family.

I had to go in for a D & C as my body would not naturally miscarry. My friend Cindy, with whom I become close over the past year, drove me to the hospital and offered to stay with me until I went into the operating room. She also offered to stay and wait in the waiting area until after the procedure, but I told her I would be okay. Reluctantly she left but told me she would make sure Arlin was there to pick me up afterward. She's another woman full of mercy and compassion; she was a great comfort to me during that time.

As they took me into the operating room, I thought about my mother going through several of her miscarriages alone, without dad around. He was either working the graveyard shift while in residency or working the emergency room at night and on weekends to make ends meet. Arlin, too, was busy working on the farm; every day there seemed to be another crisis. So mine would have to wait. Thank God for His faithfulness and His provision.

I wasn't crying or hysterical this time; I felt it was like a quiet surrender once more. What could I do to keep a child alive and growing in my womb? Absolutely nothing. Only God can cause life to begin, to continue, and to be brought forth into this world.

Arlin was there to bring me home. We didn't say much on the ride home; both of us were exhausted. Again, my bed became my refuge. I rested for a week. Both this time and last, there were no family visits, food, cards of condolence. It was like they were afraid to address the reality of my pain. This made the healing process even more difficult; I felt uncomfortable bringing up the subject of my losses...so I didn't.

Friends from church visited, called, and brought meals. That was helpful. By this time, we had finally found our home church. That had taken two and a half years. This church felt a little like my church back in the city, with many of the members from other large cities, transplants, older couples with young children, multi-ethnic and multicultural; a place Arlin and I quickly adopted as home. I was glad to have finally found a church family here, especially at a time like this.

Chapter 24

I Can't Go Back There

Thursday, July 8, 1999

How long has it been, Lord, since we have been together where I could sit and read Your word and meditate on You? Forgive me, Lord, for running from You all this time and running to work to be busy. It's terrible how I have done that. But I have. I ran to work to run from You. Heal my heart of hurt and disappointment. I do long to have a little girl like Hannah and a little boy like Ryan. Even two children. But, Father, I pray Your will be done, and perhaps it is not for me to have them on this side. Heal my heart from the loss and make me new again.

In the beginning of August, my doctor performed a histosalapingogram to help me get pregnant faster. That's a procedure where dye is forced through the fallopian tubes to make sure they are open so an egg can travel down to the uterus. It worked. I got pregnant at the end of August! I had new hope this time. It normally took at least a year or longer to conceive between miscarriages. This was quick!

After my third miscarriage, I was officially considered a high-risk-pregnancy patient. Again, my doctor insisted I go into the hospital for a weekly sonogram and blood work, which I was more than willing to do. They were keeping an extra-close watch on me. If my levels were the least bit abnormal, they were ready to take measures to save the pregnancy.

It was October and I was eight weeks pregnant. As I read a magazine in the hospital waiting room (having taken my weekly blood tests and waiting for a sonogram), I could see the nurse approaching, and immediately became anxious. I usually got the results a day or two after taking the tests, and my mind began racing. *"This can only mean bad news."* … I was right.

The nurse told me I was miscarrying. This would be my fourth. They wanted to admit me immediately into the operating room and perform another D&C. I fought the tears and the rage that was racing through my body and said, "Oh no, I can't! I'm not going through that again!" I rushed by the nurse and ran out of the hospital.

The nurse rushed after me, "But you must go through a D&C—otherwise, you could get really sick!" I didn't turn to respond; I just kept going right out the door.

On the drive home, my tears were uncontrollable. I was angry at God and I let Him have it! "How, God, could You expect me to endure this one more time? It's not fair and I don't love You right now! In fact, I'm bordering on despising You!"

When I got home, I told Arlin the news. I had cried out every tear, so I just sat there in weary silence. It was just entirely too much for me to bear this time. It would be the fourth baby we lost. Interestingly enough, in reviewing my journals, there is never a mention of this pregnancy, the miscarriage, or the surgery. I was speaking to God, but not about any of this—at least not in writing.

My journals are my secret place. It's where all my most intimate thoughts, dreams, and desires are written, validated, and shared with God. But not this. The pain over the children and my growing disappointment in God was too uncomfortable to discuss, especially with Him. Silence again.

I knew God probably wasn't pleased with my turning away, I knew from the Word that this was an opportunity for me to cling to Him even more, but I was having none of that. Deep down I knew He understood the pain of loss. He had lost His *only* Son. In fact I'm sure He was hurting for me as He watched my agonizing reactions to His will for my life. He *is* good and everything that comes from His hand is good. That's the truth, even though the facts sometimes suggest anything but that. But at the time of yet another loss, these thoughts were far from the forefront of my mind.

I called my mom to tell her the news. She said, "Honey, you have to go to the hospital and have the D & C. You could put yourself in danger. Of course you'll go."

"*No!* I don't care if I die! I'm not going to that stupid hospital and losing one more baby! I don't care what happens to me!"

She was right, however, and I knew it. Three days later, I called the doctor's office to tell them I would have the D & C. I went in the following day for the surgery. My mother-in-law drove me to the hospital and dropped me off outside on the opposite side of the street.

"Are you sure you're okay, Deborah? Do you want me to come in?" she called after me.

"I'll be fine. It's okay, really," I called back to her as I hurried across the street and into the hospital.

When I woke up in recovery, a nurse was standing over me saying, "Honey, isn't anyone coming to pick you up? The day surgery unit is closing." I was the last patient there.

I was so embarrassed. I gave them Arlin's cell phone number and asked them to call him and tell him to come for me. Feelings of abandonment, loneliness, loss, and not belonging nearly crushed me that day. "Jesus, is this how You felt?" I whispered to myself. I closed my eyes and waited for Arlin.

Overwhelmingly, through the loss, I kept contemplating God's purpose in all of this. *I'm here to glorify God. How am I glorifying God in this?* And then I would think of His Word and remember about the other saints and what they had endured. In His creative way, God's hands were on me, molding me, shaping me— He was conforming me, little by little, into His image. This is a lifelong process I realize—although, somehow I felt like I was on the *fast* track. As I lay there waiting for Arlin, I thought,"Could we take it a bit slower please?"

There was a bright spot in my life through all this in the form of one, then two, then three little girls who lived about 1,000 feet from me. They were my nieces from Arlin's oldest sister, the Grand Poobah, the one who called the farmhouse that day to ask, "And what will you do if none of us like you or accept you? Just what do you think you will do here?" What a remarkable turn of events! Through this same sister God would bring three of my greatest joys: her daughters Courtney, Laura, and Taylor.

Courtney was about three when I moved to Mount Joy. Remarkably, children are generally oblivious to adult prejudices. That was the case with Courtney, lucky for me. This little girl loved and embraced me from the day we met. We walked to and from the farm together—at times singing songs and doing all the hand motions and chatting about things on her mind, questions she had, or observations she made. We picked strawberries together and often went shopping. She sometimes helped me with the calves and on occasion she would spend the night.

As each daughter was born and reached about the age of two, they would become my newest little friend and a source of joy. The youngest of the three has a bit of my personality if I may say so: feisty, outspoken, and demanding, which could potentially be dangerous in this community. I feel for her. And her mom!

One day, Taylor, Laura, and I went shopping. Now Laura could really care less about clothes. She prefers videos. Taylor, on the other hand, was a complete delight when shopping! She got as excited as I did about a fabulous outfit. We showed up at the fitting room with four outfits for Laura and 23 for Taylor! We just couldn't decide which ones we could do without!

The limit was three per customer in the dressing room, but it wasn't busy and we begged. I sat as Taylor went from outfit to outfit admiring herself in the mirror, approving or disapproving each one. Laura had blown through all three of hers and made her decision, then left and played among the dressing rooms.

As I watched Taylor posing for herself in the mirror, I broke out laughing so loud and said, "Oh Taylor, do you know why God created you? To make Aunt Deborah laugh!" She giggled and returned to admiring her latest look in the mirror.

A week later, Taylor was over at my house and I said enthusiastically, "Taylor, you absolutely *must* see the new pants I just got. They are *so* beautiful. I just love them!"

"Let me see them right now," she demanded. I took her to my closest and showed them to her. "Oh my word, Aunt Deborah! Let me run go wash my hands so I can touch them!" She squealed with excitement as she ran to my bathroom to wash her hands. She was four years old.

She came running back to the closest to feel the fabric. "Aunt Deborah, can you buy some of these for me? I want the shoes that match just like yours! Do you think they have my size?" she pleaded. How could I resist?

I was teasing Taylor when I said that God created her to make me laugh, I'm sure He had his own plans and purposes for this precious little girl. But I have to believe that one of his reasons was truly "to make Aunt Deborah laugh."

Chapter 25

Becky's Gift

Many couples in our church who have been through infertility have chosen the path of adoption. Several of these women have tried, on occasion, to talk to me and give me information, direction, and encouragement concerning adoption. Up to this point, I was not open to adoption; not for us, anyway.

I had been able to conceive four times. I kept hoping to conceive again, carry full term, and give birth to my own children, ones born out of the union between Arlin and me. Adoption was fine for others, but it just wasn't my choice. God was working on me…not so much for the end result, but to make me pliable in His hands through the process.

By this time in my life, I had enough history with God to be certain of one thing: God knows me better than I know myself. He knows what is best for me, even when I disagree. There were so many "altars" in my life, so many times when I begged God for certain things to happen or circumstances to transpire and then weeks, months, or years later, I would reflect and say, "Thank You God, that You didn't give me what I asked for!"

Friday, October 27, 1999
Father, Your desire must be my desire. I open my heart to adoption, Father. Place those children in my life that You desire for us to have. Help me—no matter what age. I want to do Your will and walk according to the Spirit. I know in all things You work together for the good of Arlin and me, who love You and who have been *called according to Your purpose!*

That November, after having gone through four miscarriages, I was asked to give a testimony at church about grace. I had a week to prepare for the Sunday service. As I was driving back to the farm from picking up parts for a tractor, I thought, "Now what could I *possibly* have to say about grace?"

I was coming down the hill about to go over the stone bridge around the bend from our house, when I saw a flock of Canadian geese flying overhead. I kept looking up at them, watching and thinking to myself how amazing it was that they were in perfect formation—how they knew to go south for the winter, how one would move up ahead as the lead was getting tired, then move to the back and let another take over. Who had taught them this? Who had taught them how to fly as a flock? Who gave them directions and told them when to go? How did they just… know?

It was *then* that God interrupted my thoughts and said to me, *"Isn't My creation wondrous?! If I took the time to create such a lovely creation for these creatures and for your enjoyment and gave them the accuracy to take flight so precisely, to have such order, don't you think I have every day, every detail of your life so ordered for you?"*

The reality of that truth landed in my heart and that's when healing came for me, this time—by really seeing His creation, His order, His attention to details, which seem meaningless to man, is in reality, perfection. If he gave that kind of consideration to a bird who has no soul, how much more would He do for His creation made in His very own image? I had a testimony.

Thursday, April 13, 2000

Father God, I don't know if I'm hiding sadness in my everyday life about the babies, but I can confess here: I am sad. I try not to think about it. I have given all of them to You and I don't know what else to do but to keep trusting You. This time last year I was pregnant, but did not carry to term. Your word was: "Do I bring to the moment of birth and not give delivery? Do I close up the womb when I bring to delivery?" Father, I am asking You for healthy twin boys and a girl. I am asking You to open my womb and bring to fruition the fruit of my womb—and heal my body.

In the winter of 2000, my father had been prodding me to go through Invitro Fertilization (IVF). His feeling was that if I could secure a strong pregnancy through this procedure, perhaps I could carry full term. And, he wanted me to come to Texas for the procedure. His office was next to a very successful fertility clinic. He knew one of the doctors, respected his work, and several of my friends had been successful with him.

IVF was a little too… manipulated for this community and I wasn't sure how Arlin would react to the idea. I, however, reminded him that this process was very similar to a new technology that had just begun in cow breeding called "embryo transfer," in which you choose your best heifers, harvest their eggs, fertilize them and transfer them to your best cows. This is all done by a professional veterinarian to produce the strongest offspring, which would in turn insure the best quality and quantity of milk. When I half-jokingly compared this process with the one my father was suggesting, I added, "If it's good enough for the cows, it's good enough for us!" Arlin half smiled and nodded in agreement. This would mean I would be away from Arlin and the farm for at least a month. That would be a huge sacrifice at this point. It took the two of us full-time to run the dairies. And Arlin would agree only if we did the process using a surrogate along with me; he wanted to hedge our bets. If I didn't get pregnant, at least I had a 50/50 chance that she would take and carry to term.

I asked him just where he thought we would come up with a surrogate. Should I go to the mall and walk up to women and say, "Hi, would you like to carry my babies?!" I understood his position; he was thinking like a businessman. Not just anyone would do that for you, and if you did pay for someone to be a surrogate, it could be very costly.

I was still going in for my weekly blood test. I had been undergoing extensive testing for about a year to try and find out why the miscarriages happened. One day, the nurse taking my blood at the hospital began chatting with me. She knew why I was there, and told me the story of how she was a surrogate for someone she didn't even know. She answered an ad in the newspaper. She had four of her own children and felt sorry for this other woman who couldn't have her own. She figured that if she could give life for another woman that would be an awesome miracle and gift, and she did.

I knew it wasn't a coincidence that this nurse took my blood that day. How many people sign up for that, and after birthing four of their own kids? *None!* At least no one I knew. It encouraged me that finding a surrogate was possible, and that it didn't have to be someone you knew. It could be a complete stranger!

Saturday, December 30, 2000

Dear heavenly Father, how can I come back into Your Presence when I feel like I have ignored You for months? You are so righteous, forgiving, compassionate, and I am so undeserving of You and Your love. Thank You for choosing me. I would be remiss if I didn't speak what is heavy on my heart today: children. Psalm 103:5 says that You satisfy our desires with good things so that our youth is renewed like the eagle's. I desire what You desire for us—whether no children, natural, or adoption. Whatever You want. But, Lord, should we pursue IVF? Is it Your will for us to walk through that process? Is it Your will for us to go on childless or adopt? I don't know, Lord.

The IVF process is so lengthy that I had to make up my mind by mid-January as to whether I was going to Texas to find a surrogate and go through with IVF. I did hint to a few people—not in grocery stores, but to closer friends—that I was praying about finding a surrogate... but had no bites.

When I woke up early on Friday morning, January 19, it was cold and rainy; I didn't feel like going to the barn. I had a class later that morning at the Home and Farm Center. I knew I needed to hurry and get my morning chores done so I would have time to come home, shower, dress, and make the 20-minute drive into town.

I didn't sleep well the night before. I knew that this was my deadline day to call the doctors in Texas and let them know if I was going ahead with the procedure. They needed to know so they could schedule me for the February cycle. But I had no surrogate, which meant I had to say no. Arlin didn't want to proceed without a surrogate for fear that we would risk disappointment. I was just plain depressed. Even though I had maintained earlier in our struggles with miscarriages that I would never go the IVF route, I had renewed hope that maybe, just maybe, this would be our answer. At that moment it seemed that this would not work for us either.

I asked Arlin if I could get out of my morning chores because I needed to spend time with God. He knew how disappointed I was and he agreed, without hesitation. I felt I was losing my chance to exhaust medical science on our behalf. I had a good prayer time; it was a nice chat with God. I focused on thanking Him for all His goodness to us, our health, each other, our home, clothing, food, our business, family, and friends. It helped lift the sadness a bit.

I got dressed for the class and was walking out the door when the phone rang. I hesitated to answer, but then went back in the house and picked up the phone. It was another friend named Becky, this one from Texas. We had not spoken in about eight months. She said it was important, but I couldn't imagine what it could be.

She said she didn't know where Arlin and I were on the whole baby thing, but she had been praying for me over the past couple of months. Then she said that she had something to tell me, but wasn't quite sure how to do it. Now my curiosity was at an all-time high. I said, "Becky, just say it! I'm going to be late for my class. I was headed out the door when you called."

She blurted out in her thick Texas southern accent: "Listen, I have been praying for ya'll and God told me that I'm to tell you that I am willing to carry your children for you if you want. Now you may think I'm off the deep end, but I said to God, 'If I call her in the morning and she's home and not at the barn as usual, then I'll know it's you, and I'll make the offer.' Well, I called and you're home, so I'm offerin'. Do you want me to be your surrogate? You know, carry your kids for ya?!"

I sat down to catch my breath.

What?!

Did I just hear what I thought I did? I was running late for my class so I told her I'd call her back from my cell phone on my way into town.

I hung up, raced to the car and quickly dialed her back. How I made it there safely—in the rain, on the phone, adrenaline at an all-time high—I don't know. I told her our entire story, the saga of IVF or no IVF, and Arlin's insistence on a surrogate, etc. It was God! He was fitting all of this together for us. I knew this meant that God was bringing us children. It had to!

Becky was ecstatic knowing that she did indeed hear correctly and was being obedient. With that one phone call, she signed up for quite a journey of injections, medications, probing and 'planting.' I couldn't believe how generous she was being. My mind was racing, processing all that was about to happen. At the same time, I was running into the building to make it to my class.

I didn't have time to call Arlin as I slid into my seat just in time for the first session. It was a computer class on business software for dairy farms. Just what I wanted to be concentrating on after the news I had just received—I had a surrogate!

My class ended at 3 p.m. I called Arlin and told him about Becky's morning phone call. He was in shock and disbelief. Who was this woman? He had only met Becky once before when she and her new husband Don came up to Pennsylvania right after they got married. But, Arlin didn't spend any huge amount of time getting to know her. Why would she offer to do this for us?

As he was verbally contemplating all of this, I interrupted and asked, "Arlin, is it a yes or no? Just tell me so I can call the doctors in Texas!" He was silent for a moment and then said, "Yep."

I put in a call to the doctors. They weren't sold on the surrogate idea for us, but we would deal with that later. I just wanted on the schedule for February. I was ready to get this ball rolling.

A few days later, Becky called again and said, "Now I want you to know that there's just one catch. I want you to take my son Nick (her teenage son from her first marriage) for a few weeks this summer, let him work on the farm with you, and put a work ethic in him." Okay, do we look like the OK Corral Ranch for juvenile rehab? But, hey, the lady was willing to carry my kids for nine months, the least I could do was take hers for a couple of weeks. I agreed.

Over the next few days and weeks, many questions covered the pages of my journals. Questions ranging from, "Is this the way You have chosen to give us children?" to "Do both Becky and I get implanted so I end up with an instant family of five or more?" And of course in the back of my mind: Will we get any children at all from this?

The doctors weren't sure which of us should be implanted. A woman of my age normally only ended up with one or two good embryos. The question then was, if there were only one or two embryos, which one of us would have the better chance of carrying a healthy baby to term? Arlin opted for Becky since she had three of her own children with healthy pregnancies and problem-free birth experiences. But I wasn't sure how I felt about that. I knew one thing for sure; our primary purpose was to have our children, no matter whose body they grew in.

I flew to Texas to begin the drug protocol. We were off to a great start when my body responded better to the drugs than anticipated. Everything looked more than wonderful. The stats were above normal for the amount of eggs they retrieved, the amount that fertilized, and the amount of good embryos that formed. They harvested 18 eggs, 12 of them fertilizing. After a couple days of incubation, we had ten strong and promising embryos. The next step was the implantation.

When Becky and I went in for the procedure, they told us the good news. But the doctors also cautioned that embryos formed with "older" eggs harvested from a woman my age didn't usually survive the thawing process. So there was no reason to only implant a couple in each of us and freeze the remainder for another try, which had been my plan. I thought at least I would have another chance just in case neither of us became pregnant. I knew a couple of women whose first attempt at IVF failed, but who tried again a year or two later with embryos that had been frozen—and had success!

The doctors advised me to have all ten implanted, five in Becky and five in me. The success rate was generally 30 percent for women going through IVF to become pregnant, and about 20 percent to carry to term. That wasn't favorable, and the percentage rates drop for every year after 40. So it looked like an all-or-nothing proposition. We were going for all.

Becky was in another room awaiting my decision. I asked the doctor to ask her if she was willing to have five implanted. He returned with a hesitant look on his face. Becky was clearly a little freaked out by the idea. Carrying one or two babies was the maximum she had in mind, but five?! The doctor told me Becky was making a phone call to her husband. I waited on pins and needles (well, maybe just needles) for his response.

The doctor came back in with a direct quote from Becky's husband, Don. "What the heck. Put in all five. What do you have to lose?"

I don't know for sure, but I can only imagine Becky's response being, "Yeah, easy for you to say! You don't have to carry them!"

So it was decided: the doctors implanted five embryos in Becky and five in me. This was hedging our bets to the max. During the procedure, the doctors said to me, "You know, you'd better start thinking big!"

"What do you mean?" I asked, preoccupied with my uncomfortable mid-procedure position.

"Do you realize you could possibly come out of this with ten children? So, think mini-van, bigger house, someone to help you get your babies back to Pennsylvania." Oh, my. The ride was just beginning.

Chapter 26

God, I Don't Understand...

I was thrilled at the prospect of an instant family! Okay, not ten all at once, but I was ready for the best scenario. Everything was pointing in the right direction. The reports from the doctors and nurses all along the way were favorable—in fact, more than favorable. The outcome seemed certain: children. It was just a question of how many.

Becky and I both went home to my parents' house for bed rest the remainder of the day. Then, Becky returned to her home, but we agreed we'd both spend the next week on bed rest to insure implantation. Every day, we spoke back and forth on the phone wondering how many babies we were carrying, what the sexes would be, how long I would stay in Texas before traveling back to Pennsylvania with the babies, in utero. This was a once in a lifetime event for both of us, a shared experience that was unusual, to say the least. We couldn't help but be giddy with excitement, anticipation, and great expectations!

Toward the end of the week, Becky and I decided to venture out to lunch with my mom and sister. While at cafe, though, Becky started feeling faint and very warm. She quickly padded the back of her neck and her face with a cloth napkin drenched in cold water. She tried to recompose herself, but said she still felt nauseous. This was music to my ears—of course 'feeling nauseous' could only mean one thing; she was pregnant!

We went to my sister Jean's husband's dental office to give Becky oxygen. She sat in the chair, with Rick giving her oxygen until she recovered. Becky admitted that she had 'cheated' and taken a pregnancy test that was faintly positive. We were told not to take a test because we could get a false negative if we took it too early. But, this news confirmed it for me. All was good. As far as we knew, Becky was now carrying one or more of our babies!

Of course, in a split second, a wave of depression washed over me. I hadn't had any signs of pregnancy, at all. Did this mean that only Becky would carry my babies and I would not carry any? I began to cry out of self pity.

My sister Jean got annoyed with me and said, "How can you be so ungrateful?! At least one of you got pregnant. It's still your baby no matter where it grows, just be glad!" Okay, so I needed a quick attitude adjustment. I just longed to be pregnant, to carry life— my baby, inside of me. But a healthy baby; our baby, Arlin's and mine – that was what was important and all I really wanted. So it really didn't matter who ultimately carried the child: attitude adjustment complete.

A couple of days later, we went in for our blood tests. We left the clinic and waited for the results. We were told they would call within a few hours. I remember it so clearly. Becky and I went over to Jean's house, and then went next door to visit a neighbor. We were sitting at her kitchen table; chatting and watching the children play in the yard when my cell phone rang.

When I answered the phone, I could hear the incredulity in the nurse's voice as she said, "Deborah, I have to tell you… I'm just so, so sorry, but neither you nor Becky is pregnant. I am so sorry… We were just sure that at least one of you would have taken. I am so sorry, Deborah."

Here I was, sitting at the kitchen table of an acquaintance, hearing this devastating news. They, I'm sure, guessed from the look on my face, that it was bad news, but I went ahead and told them the results. My sister Jean was in shock. I was frozen. I couldn't cry; I couldn't scream or yell; I had to remain composed. After all, I was in her friend's home. Immediately, I asked if we could leave; I wanted to go home.

There were no words to explain the horror of learning that news. My mind revisited every sonogram I had and hearing the dreadful words, "…no heartbeat," no baby. This couldn't be! Not *this* time. Why the surrogate at the last minute?! Why the positive response to the drug protocol, the large number of eggs, the number of good embryos, the optimistic doctors and nurses? For what? God, please, tell me why!

Arlin was arriving by plane from Pennsylvania that afternoon. He wasn't able to get an earlier flight into San Antonio. I was hoping to not receive any news until after he arrived, but it was too late.

Becky and I drove together in silence to the airport to pick up Arlin. Becky stayed at security and let me go to meet Arlin alone. It was a long walk to the gate. I kept wondering how to break the news to him, what to say. The last he had heard, Becky was pregnant for sure, and I was waiting for the blood test.

I stood there, alone, waiting for him as he came off the plane. He had that familiar million dollar smile on his face, believing we had good news. He ran up to hug me, excited that we were pregnant.

I couldn't hold it in any longer. I blurted out the blood tests results and that there would be no children. Arlin's smile fell as he dropped his bags and leaned against the wall. "You're not serious… I thought you told me Becky did a test and it was positive?"

"She did, and she thought it was positive. But, we both had our blood tests that undeniably confirmed we're not pregnant."

We both stood there looking at each other in disbelief and despair. Finally, Arlin grabbed me and we just held each other. I began to weep, quietly, in his arms. We were in the middle of the airport and I didn't want to draw unwanted attention or make a scene. I was devastated but was comforted that Arlin was finally with me.

Becky dropped us off at my parents' house. I didn't want to start crying again; I was afraid I wouldn't stop. Arlin and I had a glass of wine and went straight to bed. It was three o'clock in the afternoon. It was a bright, warm, beautiful sunny day. We closed the blinds and prayed for sleep to overtake us. We needed the escape; I just didn't want to feel anything.

Bless her heart, my mother came upstairs to try and comfort me with 'words of wisdom' about God's ultimate plan. I told her, "Mom, I can't talk about it. And I don't want to hear about God and His sovereignty, right now. He thinks He can just emotionally jerk me around like this and expect me to survive it. Sure, just keep putting the carrot out there, have me chase it, and right before I grab it say, 'Just kidding,' and yank it away from me! Forget it! I wouldn't treat my worst enemy this way! I hate Him!" I buried my head in the pillow, muffling my cries.

Mom quietly left the room and I finally fell asleep, Arlin beside me.

I didn't want to wake up. I knew that when I did, I would have to face it again. It wouldn't have just been a dream. I would have to feel the excruciating pain of disappointment all over again. There were no more tears to cry, and there was no more strength left to endure another loss. There would be no picking myself up by my bootstraps this time, nor would I run to God for mercy and grace. In my mind, there was nowhere left to go. And Arlin couldn't fix it either.

I had finally hit a wall and I had nothing in me to take me over it. I was done. I knew that ignoring God wasn't the answer, but I couldn't help it; I was furious with Him. He's God, He could handle it.

I became painfully aware of my insignificance. I'm just this blade of grass down here; a single, fragile stalk of irrelevance. Why should my desire to have children have any influence on God? Maybe He is not mindful of me at all. Even as I thought this, I knew it wasn't true, but I felt as if it was.

Soon after, Arlin returned to Pennsylvania. He had to get back to the farm, but I wasn't ready. I stayed with my parents a bit longer. Thank God for my family and friends in Texas who stood by me through another loss ... I was comforted by their kindness for the days I was there.

It was hard to understand why all the circumstances looked so good—why Becky had offered to be a surrogate, why I had such good test results with the drugs and the procedure—why God had allowed all this, and still… no babies.

I was beginning to really relate to Job. He just wanted to curse the day he was born—and then die. But God said to him, "Who are you to question Me?" I realized God was right…Who *am* I to question God? Was I around when He formed the earth from a void, placed the seas and oceans and set their boundaries, placed the stars in heaven, and all the rest of the stuff God did to get this show on the road? No, I was not.

However, just because you know the truth, it doesn't make it any easier to accept. I needed time to process and grieve.

The last entry in my 2000 journal was March 18th, a couple of days after receiving the news. I jotted down a quick prayer of protection for Arlin, on his journey back to Pennsylvania, for wisdom, glory, knowledge of God, and to have his heart drawn to Him. In another words, I was talking to God about someone else, but *not* about me. Eventually, I stopped talking to God altogether; I didn't have a secret place with Him anymore...

Chapter 27

All the Way from Russia

I arrived home to Pennsylvania at the end of March and was immediately presented with an adoption opportunity. Or should I say, a "challenge" to adopt. My friend Joyce and her husband had adopted two sweet little girls—sisters—from Russia, although not without a huge struggle and astronomical cost. She had also gone through infertility for eight years, and then finally turned to adoption at the age of thirty. I think she felt my pain and always had me in her thoughts, so that when an adoption opportunity crossed her path, she immediately thought of me. She received a phone call from a friend about a family of three coming to America from Russia, in need of a home.

Joyce pushed for Arlin and me to consider adopting them. She did the hard sell, describing the children and detailing the extent of their need. But I'd barely landed from Texas and my heartbreak was still fresh; I was in no mood to open my mind or heart to another complicated scenario. I told her in no uncertain terms: I was *not* considering adoption.

Besides, my infertility issues were different. I had been pregnant four times; it wasn't that I couldn't conceive, it was just that I couldn't seem to sustain a pregnancy. I was not willing to give up on my hope of giving birth. I wasn't against adoption for anyone else, but I just didn't care for that option for us.

Joyce was persistent in saying that we would be the ideal couple with the ideal situation. It was a sibling group of two girls and a boy, ages ten, twelve, and fourteen. "What better place than a farm to raise children?!" she kept telling us. The children had been separated from each other after being removed from their parents at a young age. They were being reunited for the first time in five years and coming to the U.S.

I kept telling her, *"No,* I'm not interested!" But she kept insisting we should at least meet the children. "What harm could it do to just meet them?" she asked. This went on for a couple of months.

I still wasn't journaling. I didn't have much to say to God. Somehow, writing our conversations, my prayers, and my feelings and emotions on paper makes them *permanent.* It's an odd feeling, but they become inescapable. I wasn't ready to have the volatility of my emotions immortalized on paper.

I had asked Arlin his thoughts on several occasions about meeting the children. Finally, in July of that summer, Arlin agreed. His exact words were, "What could it hurt to just meet them?" So just three months after my IVF experience, Arlin and I agreed to meet the Russian children. We took along another couple from our church that had also been going through infertility for the past *ten* years. They had just begun to consider adoption. We felt the least we could do was to provide another option for these kids since we weren't feeling like we were a viable choice. We were only 'just meeting' them.

The four of us had a lively discussion on our drive over to meet the children. I said to Ralph and Leanne, "Hey, we're glad you guys are along. Perhaps this is the answer to your family situation. You both work with children; you're open to adoption, so this must be for you!"

"Well, how do you know this isn't for you? Think of all the instant help you would have on the farm, Arlin! We're curious about the children, but we're mainly going to support you," Leanne replied.

We arrived at Tom and Mary's, where the children were staying for three weeks. The plan was for Tom and Mary to find them a home then the children would return to Russia, and the adoption proceedings would begin.

Tom and Mary had four birth children, but they had been moved through a series of events to adopt the two sisters from Russia. In the process of adopting their girls, Mary met a little girl named Ida, who was best friends with one of her newly adopted daughters, Tina. Ida and Tina had lived in the same orphanage together, and Tina desperately wanted an American family living in the same area to adopt her best friend, Ida, so they could stay close. This scenario involved finding Ida's older sister and brother who were each at their own orphanages. After locating the older siblings, Mary and Tom then had to get permission to bring all three children to the States, fly them here, and find them a forever family. This was all done privately and at the expense of Tom and Mary. They were determined to find these children parents to complete their family and we were identified as a strong possibility.

Mary brought these three beautiful children before us. What happened next was something almost indescribable.

All my life, moving in different Christian circles, I have seen the miraculous happen for others, but I have never experienced anything physically manifested in myself. I used to wonder why others had these physical reactions or experiences of the Holy Spirit and I didn't. I had my own experiences with God, but nothing tangible—until now.

Mary brought the children out to meet us. The children were told that we were just some friends coming over to visit with the hosts. Tom and Mary didn't want the children to feel they were being "shopped." That was a wise idea. They feared if the children took an immediate liking to a couple and then the couple rejected them, it would be heartbreaking for them.

We were sitting on their porch at the picnic table, the six of us. I had an attitude right off the bat. *What are Arlin and I doing here? There is no chance that we're adopting anyone, much less an entire sibling group! Let's get real here, folks!* I thought I was only doing my civic duty to meet the children.

Then the three children came outside to meet us. As they were being introduced, I *physically* felt this wave of—I don't know quite how to explain it—but it wasn't just intellectual or emotional, it was like…well…the perfect analogy is when you are out in the ocean and you swim beyond the breakers. You're just floating out there where the surges and swells of water form the next wave. As the next beginnings of a wave surges through you, this mound of water lifts you up and gently lets you down—and you know that's the next wave forming. That's *exactly* what I felt coming over my body and my heart— these waves of…longing? … love? I wasn't sure. All I knew was that it was something powerful! I could feel it!

Instantly, I said in my heart, *God, You're changing me right now, aren't You?! You know that I am dead set against adopting. But here You are, changing my heart right this instant and placing a love in it for these kids. You want me to say yes, right? Oh Lord, I can tell, I can tell! And I can't stop it! Well, You just can't do that! I will not love them and I will not adopt!* My attitude was obstinate and rebellious. Not good…

Try and stop the ocean swells as the next wave comes in. It's impossible. And so was the change happening to me at that moment, right then as I was sitting at that picnic table. I was being carried away, wave by wave. Inside if felt like a time bomb full of conflicting emotions. The children stayed only about ten more minutes, but after they went back into the house, I asked a million questions. It seemed as if I couldn't ask quickly enough, nor could Mary or Tom keep up with the answers. Do you put them in public school as non-English-speaking kids, or do you home-school? What if they don't like you after a while? What if you don't like *them* after a while? What if they get homesick? What if they hate the farm? Do we need to learn Russian? When can we have them? Can we re-name them, or do we keep their Russian names? On and on the questions flew.

We asked questions on a personal level regarding how their own adoption experience had gone, what their most difficult struggles had been, and what obstacles, adjustments, disappointments, joys, and surprises there were. They patiently fielded our questions and added some of their own we didn't know to ask. They knew because they had been there.

Overwhelmingly, though, they communicated that "none of the pains, the difficulties, or the struggles could outweigh the joy we have received in taking these two girls into our home and having them become a part of our family! It's just something words cannot express!" That was it. I wanted those children.

The drive home was pretty quiet. The four of us were occupied by our own thoughts, considering what had just happened. I was afraid that Ralph and Leanne wanted the children. I asked them if they felt inclined to adopt these kids. My mind was screaming, "No! Please, no." But part of me was secretly hoping they would say yes, so I wouldn't have to submit myself to the emotional roller coaster of the adoption process. Admittedly, I was afraid. This meant instant family. Could I handle that? Would I be a good mother? "I don't know about this, three at one time and two almost-teenagers?!"

Finally, Leanne said they didn't feel inclined to adopt the children. They were younger and really interested in adopting an infant. Right after that, Ralph said, "Isn't it amazing that the 14-year-old boy looks exactly like Arlin?" Leanne chimed in, agreeing, "He could be your son, Arlin!" I needed to hear that like I needed a hole in my head!

My thoughts kept racing ahead of me. Could I do this? Could I adopt three siblings? Who didn't speak English at ages 10, 12, and 14? What was Arlin thinking? Had he felt anything? Could he handle this? Why isn't he saying anything?

Sitting at the table that night, I didn't tell Arlin what had happened to me. We arrived home and simply went to bed, without discussing what we had just experienced. We were both in our own worlds of thought wondering what God had planned. I may not have listened to Him much lately, but I wasn't a fool. I knew He had His hand in everything, including this. What might He be up to now?

I didn't mention a word to Arlin regarding the children the following day. I didn't want to influence his decision. He had to be the one to bring it up; I knew that much after being with this man for almost nine years. Arlin came in from the farm that night and still said nothing. I couldn't take it anymore. Finally, I "nonchalantly prodded, "What are you thinking?

He replied, "You tell me first."

I began to smile and told him everything I experienced while meeting the children. I told him how I felt my heart changing and an inexplicable love sweep over me. Then he held up his hand, smiling and he interrupted with, "I wanted your decision to be my confirmation—because I felt the same way! I believe those are our kids. Did you see how amazing it was that Erick looks exactly like me?" It was a done deal; we were adopting those children!

We planned to have the children come stay with us on the farm for a few days the following week. We began to get everything ready. We told both our families that we were adopting a sibling group from Russia. Everyone on Arlin's side was enthusiastic. My folks were a little hesitant, though. My mother, knowing me, said, "Are you sure you can handle this? You aren't exactly the most patient person and you don't handle crises very well. What if one of them gets hurt or has a farming accident and you can't communicate with them?"

Let me explain how mother thinks—and, fortunately or not, how I think, as I'm sure I inherited a bit of her rationale.

Around the time when Arlin and I had just gotten married, I looked out of my bedroom window one morning and saw this guy walking across our yard dressed in army fatigues. He had black paint on his face, sported a ponytail, carried a rifle, and had a chair *tied to his back!*

"Oh my God! What or who the heck was that who just walked past my bedroom window?!" I screamed on the phone to Arlin.

"Oh that's just Bill, our neighbor. He's probably out hunting deer. No worry. He's a cool guy."

"A cool guy? What?! Are you nuts?! He looks like he's ready to hop a chopper to Desert Storm or something. What if he shoots, misses, and kills one of our kids in the driveway, or hits the trailer and kills me?" I shouted in panic.

"What?! We don't even have any kids yet! And he won't hit the trailer— he's a good shot. He doesn't aim that way anyway. He'll shoot away from the trailer. What are you all hyped up about? My word, don't you have something better to do?"

I immediately hung up and called my mother. I described this crazy person crossing my property, and the first thing she said was, "What if he shoots one of your kids while they're playing in the driveway or he hits you in your trailer?!" Clearly, I am my mother's daughter.

Arlin had gone out looking for a house to buy near the farm, as our mobile home was too small to accommodate three more people. I had picked out bedding for the girls' room, planned Erick's room, called schools, and organized schedules to accommodate three children into our lives! In short, I was way down the road, emotionally.

We had visions of Erick on the tractor sitting next to his dad, driving the tractor and bailing hay—and the girls feeding calves with mom, bringing food to the guys while they were harvesting. They were wonderful thoughts, and we couldn't wait to begin out lives with our new family.

On Friday I called and asked if we could pick up the children early, as we couldn't wait until Sunday. What I heard on the other end of the line was the ultimate wound to my heart...

Chapter 28

The First Shall Be Last

Mary's voice was tense, "Well…now there's a glitch. She said with a sigh, "You see, there are other families interested, and unfortunately you're not first on the list. The first family has gone on vacation for ten days, during which time they will be deciding whether or not they are going to adopt the children. We'll have to wait until they return for their answer. Then we will go from there."

What?!

Out of sheer incredulity, I mumbled some response and as quickly as possible, got off the phone. I immediately called my friend from church that knew this couple and set up this whole scenario, and tried to get some answers. My mind was clearer by this time and I asked her point blank, "Didn't you tell me we were the children's only hope and the only ones interested in these kids? We would have never agreed to meet them if this was going to be handled like an auction!"

She was aghast. She didn't know of any other families. She called Mary and then called me back immediately. "I'm so sorry, Deborah. I don't understand. You *were* the only ones. I don't know who these other families are! I don't understand what's happening; this wasn't what I was told. Look, we'll just have to wait and pray. I believe with all my heart you and Arlin are the best choice for these kids. What could be better for children than to be raised on a farm surrounded by family? Let's just pray."

I was beside myself. I hung up the phone and gave in to tears. Before, I had always cried for children I didn't yet know. This time, the children I cried for had names; they had faces. How could this be happening? What a tortuous turn of events. I was now in a state of anguish, which was quickly turning into anger. Who did this couple think they were, to torment us like this? There was nothing I could do but wait, hope, and pray. I knew this, but my emotions were flying, the rage building—not to mention the anxiety. My mind was constantly trying to calculate the "what ifs" and the variety of possible outcomes.

The next ten days went by ever so slowly. I finally got up the nerve to call on Saturday. I was at the barn, feeding the calves. I felt such a protective (dare I say it), maternal response to these four-legged creatures. They were so wobbly and innocent, and completely dependent on me as I fed each one her morning bottle. I felt a little silly for how much affection I had for these furry little babes; my only outlet for my innate mothering instincts.

I finally built up some courage and called Mary about the children. Mary said, "The couple has returned and decided to take the children."

Tears stung my eyes. I walked out of the barn to find a more private place to talk. The milker was in the barn and the other workers were busy with their various tasks, but all were within earshot. I needed fresh air and wide open spaces to take in this information.

I looked out over the corn fields, so beautiful in the morning sun; everything looked so fresh and hopeful at the break of day. It was the exact antithesis of what I was feeling. I finally spoke, "But, you promised them to us; you had us meet them; you tried convincing us to adopt; you said no one else was in the running—that we were their only hope—and now you're telling me we can't have them?!" She apologized profusely, still without explanation, and then ended the call.

The moments after that call are still a blur, but I do remember falling to my knees outside the calf hutches, burying my head in my grubby hands, and just breaking down. "How could this be? These were *our* children. God, how can she just take them away? It's not fair, it's just not fair," I cried. I called Arlin from my cell phone and gave him the news. Silence. Yet another time we had to grieve the loss, each time with fewer answers and more questions… for God.

The following day, Sunday, I couldn't get out of bed nor did I want to… ever again. I just wanted to sleep. There's no pain when I'm sleeping. Arlin suggested that we drive to Cape May for an escape of sorts. It was a painfully quiet ride there. We drove around, looked at houses, watched people, and went for lunch. Not much was said. There wasn't much we could say to one another. I tried not to cry. I tried to "snap out of it," to accept it, to move on. Arlin was very quiet.

On the way home I said to him, "Are you still talking to God? And if so, how could you? Can you believe what He allowed to come into our lives and at this time? It's mental manipulation; one minute you're pregnant, the next you're not; one minute you have a surrogate, the next…no babies; one minute you have three beautiful children to adopt, the next…just kidding! How many times, Arlin, can God expect me to go through this emotional roller coaster? I wasn't looking to adopt. It came to us! How could God do this to us?!"

Very calmly he said, "God is still good, Deborah, no matter what you're feeling or what has happened to us. He is good. Look at all your blessings. Don't say that He's not good! He is." At that moment I was definitely Job's wife. I wanted to say, "Let's just curse God and die." I was so resentful at Arlin for not being mad at God. But he wasn't, plain and simple.

At that moment I saw the treasure God had given me in Arlin. His complete trust in God was so pure, and my admiration for him was unlike anything else I had experienced before. This man was in as much pain over the loss as I was, even more so in some way. He had been so looking forward to having a son to work alongside him on the farm, one that even looked like him! But, he refused to curse God. He refused to charge God with anything but goodness. I was in awe…what an amazing man. He loves God no matter what.

The next morning, around 3 a.m., I woke up brushing something off my mouth. I turned on the light and saw a large black spider on my pillow. "Arlin!" I screamed. "Look what's on my pillow! Quick! Kill it!" I had a major aversion to spiders, anyway—and this one was on my mouth!

Arlin was half asleep and didn't know what all the fuss was about. I just couldn't wait for him, so I quickly killed the nasty looking thing by snatching it up with a Kleenex. I flushed it down the toilet and went back to bed, but I still had the heebie-jeebies thinking about that thing being on my face. And then I felt God speak: *Deborah, you opened the door to the enemy by cursing Me, so the enemy had grounds to taunt you. You must repent immediately for cursing Me with your mouth. Because of your sin, that's the very thing Satan attacked.*

I lay there in shock. I felt ashamed, instantly, for my irreverence to God and my lack of trust in His ultimate plan. God revealed Himself, yet again. He's still in charge and He's still in control—so who was I to curse Him? I'm just a mere human who's only on this earth a short while. I repented. I was trembling at the realization that I had gone that far. In my pain, my heart had grown cold and hard against God and I justified my right to dismiss the creator of the Universe, who was also my heavenly father. I wasn't running to my Daddy God for healing, but away from Him to shield my pain, hurt, and bitterness. I now realized that was emotional suicide. And in an instant, my heart was turned back to Him.

Even though God had brought me through another devastating loss, I still had to heal. I had to forgive. I had lots of questions for God, lots of tears, and plenty of my own opinions about what should occur in my life. Arlin was disappointed, but in general, he's not one for showing much emotion. We rarely discussed it. He was processing what had happened in his way, and I in mine.

Monday, August 13, 2001

Well, Father, last Monday, we spent time with the children and decided to adopt them, and this Friday, we were told we couldn't…it was a tremendous week. I know that You changed our hearts—at least I think You did—and that You are disciplining me harshly. From the very start of our desire and pursuit of family, it feels like You have dangled carrots and pulled the rug out from under us time and time again: four miscarriages, the IVF and surrogate, and now the children from Russia. From my perspective, You want to break my will and get me to a point of surrender with You. I guess I want to ask that You would do it gently and lovingly, just as "The Horse Whisperer" broke that hurting horse and knew the only way to do so was not with force, but love. I don't understand Your ways with me; they seem to be so harsh. But I do *understand now that You can do with me as You please. I know who You are and about Your sovereignty and Your power. And I do understand that I have to bow down to Your throne. What else do You want to teach me?*

Have mercy on Arlin and me and lead us through a season of peace, rest, joy, and fulfillment. Don't You think we need a reprieve from the struggle? Could You send a host of angels to come and do spiritual battle for us and give us a breather? You led Arlin and me together for Your purpose, but without You and Your Mighty help, forget it—because we can't do anything! As it says in Psalm 105, God, You are God, most certainly. Please forgive me for being angry with You and help me to understand You and to trust You, again. This is where I most need Your help. I do not understand and/or trust, lest I would not fret, which only leads to evil.

Tuesday, December 6, 2001

Father, Son, and Holy Spirit, I thank You now and today for not bringing those three children into our lives. There is no way I could handle them, feed them, etc., and work full-time for my husband. I don't understand why it is so important to have this farm business, but You have given this to us, and I surrender and submit to Your will.

At this point, I accepted that children were not part of God's plan for our lives, and it didn't matter why. What was important was the fact that I needed to face the truth and move on. That truth, however, was somewhat fragmented. I could acknowledge that, for now, adoption wasn't an option, or IVF, or a surrogate. But as long as I was ovulating and had the ability to conceive, I knew that every month until I hit menopause I would continue to wonder… and hope. I would always question if I was pregnant and if so, whether or not I would be able to carry to term.

But I haven't conceived since.

PART THREE

NO BABIES...
NO CAREER...
NO WAY I'M STAYING HERE!

My flesh and my heart may fail,
but God is the strength of my heart and my portion forever.
(Psalm 73:26)

Chapter 29

Farm Living

Arlin had been farming since he was old enough for his foot to reach the tractor pedal. That's all he knew. Shortly after we got engaged, he secretly hoped that when we married, I would insist we move back to New York or somewhere else far, far away where he could escape the all-consuming life of farming. He was physically and mentally exhausted from the relentless grind of owning, operating and managing a dairy farm. He often said, "I feel like I'm ready to retire and I'm only thirty-one!"

He was increasingly frustrated because he had no way of expanding the dairy physically or growing his business, financially. The barns were (and still are) old bank barns that were carved into the side of a hill back in the 1950's. This meant he was sort of boxed in, geographically; there was nowhere to go. The hill was on one side, and a busy road on the other. Perhaps he could have chosen another site somewhere else on the farm, but the way the land was configured and for other logistical reasons, it wasn't an option.

I knew that Arlin had a gift for farming, but he didn't seem happy doing it as his life's work. He was frustrated and felt he was facing a dead end. He was really wrestling with whether or not he should stay in the dairy business.

Our situation has often been called "dairymen's purgatory", which means the business is too small to support hiring more employees, but too large for the work to be done by the owner. Arlin had a hired man, but the farm was too much for just Arlin and him to handle.

So, that spring, we made a commitment to prayer regarding Arlin's future in agriculture and whether or not he should make a career move. We prayed earnestly for three months that God would direct Arlin's steps in the specific area of his career. In addition, we traveled to New York, Washington D.C., and Baltimore, where Arlin met with successful businessmen referred to us by close friends and family. With each businessman, he discussed the pros and cons and plausibility of a career move.

I remember one of the conversations Arlin had with my dad concerning our present situation and the prospects of a career change. Dad said, "Arlin, what do you really want to do? What is your dream? You know, I went to Texas with a wife, five small children, a hundred dollars to my name, and a dream. Even though it was a struggle, we were happy. It's no use being miserable; go for what you dream." What was Arlin's dream? I was about to find out.

After all his searching and praying, one day Arlin came to me and said, "Honey, I believe God wants us to work together, side by side, full-time on the farm."

There was a long moment of silence as I stared, deer in the headlights, at my husband. When I found my voice, I said "Okay, but weren't we praying about a career move for *you*? How did we get from 'career move for Arlin' to 'Deborah full-time on the farm'? And if that's what you heard, just exactly what do you have in mind for me to do?" I was still waiting and praying for God to open another door, perhaps in New York City. I certainly wasn't hearing "Deborah on the farm, full-time, part-time or even a summer internship," that's for sure!

"Farming," he said. "We need to work full-time together… on the dairy farm…farming." Well, what in the world would I do on the farm—and hello? Did the thought ever occur to him that perhaps I wasn't *looking* for a full-time job *on the farm* and that was not exactly my dream?

"Call your agents in New York City and Philly and tell them you're out. No more auditioning, commercials, trade shows, or anything," he said quite convincingly. "And then you'll start working full-time with me."

I felt the heat rise from the middle of my back to the top of my neck. I was still too young for hot flashes, so I recognized this as plain old anger on the rise. "And just what am I going to do on a dairy farm, Arlin? I know nothing about cows, farming, fieldwork, or anything!" He said he wasn't sure yet, but he'd figure it out. What he did feel certain about was that we needed to work together and become a team in farming—he told me not to worry about what I was going to do, "There's *never* a lack of work on a dairy farm!"

How very reassuring. Oh, I had no doubt he'd find *something* for me to do. I was just certain I wouldn't be wearing my designer shoes while doing it…

Friday, March 6, 1998

Lord God, Father, help me to gracefully pull out of my agents and leave acting behind. It is so hard for me—because I feel like a failure. I guess I have to die to the dream of acting because You have another dream for me. You have another place for me, and I must step into that place. But…I am not prepared…and I'm not thrilled, either.

Arlin started me out "gradually" with feeding calves. We milked 150 cows at that time, so I had to feed between ten to 20 calves twice a day. Not a huge amount of work to begin with. When calves are first born, they're vulnerable and need a lot of loving care. And they were so cute! They needed love, attention, and someone with a mothering, nurturing spirit to care for them. Lord knows, I had plenty of that to go around, so I quickly adapted to this job. Having *something* to mother was good for me, and they were snuggly cute.

Arlin taught me how to feed them. The newborns got two bottles (four quarts) a day of their mother's milk, along with a tiny bit of grain and water. Next was changing the bedding, which happened daily to keep the calves dry. It's what I call their "diaper change."

Little by little, Arlin taught me more and more, not just about calves, but about cows, milking, feed, equipment, soil, and crops ad infinitum! I quite *naturally* became the "go fetch" person for anyone and everyone on the farm. That meant I had to learn my way around town…

They have a funny way of giving directions in this county. Seems like they don't like to give distances, road names, or any kind of directional clues; it's more like, "Do you know where the Smuckers or the Muellers live? Well, go up to their place, take a right, go up to the crossroads 'til you get to Erisman Mennonite Church. Go left, then up there a ways you'll come to where the Horsts live. Follow that road for a bit—the road curves to the left—and just over the bridge there's a schoolhouse. Turn in there, drive in around the back, and look for someone named Mike." *What?!*

I took many a scenic route on my way to 'fetch' things; in fact, I still do. The most *creative* directions I ever got were: "Go down to the Buck—*never mind how to get there*—and then as you're going down the hill, which is a two-lane highway, just over a bridge you'll see a road. Turn right. Follow that road around awhile; you'll go over a covered bridge and pass a few farms. As soon as you see an Amish farm with a white barn on the left—*oh, now I know exactly which farm it is, on account of the white barn and all*—go in there, follow the lane around back, and ask for Ed."

An hour and a half later…when I finally did find the correct lane from the two-lane highway, I stopped every Amish man named Samuel, Benjamin, and Noah I found and asked, "Where's the place that sells the mobile home tires?" Eventually, I made my way to the *right* Amish farm and found Ed. It was the lane that went *behind* the house that was across from the stream that was to the left of the white barn to the right of the barnyard! Thank God I'm not afraid to ask.

Meanwhile, we kept having more and more heifer calves and the herd kept growing. "Wait a minute," I thought. "Weren't we praying for an open door away from here?" We had nowhere to put those extra cows. Maybe God wanted us to sell out on the high end, with more animals. That would help us get a new start somewhere else. I was just sure God had a new career for Arlin *elsewhere*. But until then, we kept adjusting, somehow, to the number of cows coming into the herd and we persisted in prayer. My prayers were often focused on a way out of farming.

Tuesday, June 16, 1998

Father, why did these two agents call in one day? Do I go or not?

Roll your works upon the Lord [commit and trust them wholly to Him; He will cause your thoughts to become agreeable to His will, and so shall your plans be established and succeed.... The lot is cast into the lap, but the decision is wholly of the Lord [even the events that seem accidental are really ordered by Him]. (Proverbs 16:3, 33, AMP)

Father, do You want me to have children? I know Your blessings come when You are ready. Speak to me about this, because I cannot see now. My eyes and heart are dulled to the vision and dream. I am trying to be the best wife I can be—the best farmer's wife. You must continue to show me the way.

I was desperately searching for any reason to stay in farming. And what was about to happen would make me search even harder.

Arlin visited with a neighboring farmer named Sam Jacobs, to tell him he would no longer be renting Sam a piece of equipment. Arlin had recently sold the piece and he wanted Sam to know so he could find another resource. In the course of their conversation, Sam mentioned to Arlin that he was selling off one of his several farms and asked Arlin if he would be interested in buying it. The farm was crop and pastureland with an old bank barn, but no dairy. Arlin said no.

But Arlin did mention to Sam he would be interested in buying his dairy farm if Sam ever decided to sell it. Well, of course, Sam just laughed. He had four sons and one of them was his main herdsman who had his own cows. Farms like this were generational businesses and very rarely left the family of origin. But God was moving.

Two days later, I was in the milk house cleaning out calf bottles when a farmer I didn't recognize came in looking for Arlin. I introduced myself as Arlin's wife and inquired if I could help. He said he was our neighbor, Sam, who had rented equipment from us. (We lived adjacent to one another, but I had never personally met him.) He asked if Arlin was seriously interested in buying his dairy because he was interested in selling! I dropped my jaw, the bottles, and the scrub brush and said, "Just a moment, I'll get him for you."

I called Arlin on the radio and told him Sam was looking for him. Arlin came by the barn, gave me a quick smile, and he and Sam drove off together in Arlin's truck. While they were gone, I kept working, burning with curiosity at what buying another dairy would possibly mean for us. Truly, Sam couldn't be serious about selling his dairy…and Arlin couldn't be serious about buying it…could he?

Arlin returned and said, "I think we're buying Sam's dairy farm." Before I could respond, he continued, "Now Deborah, I don't want you talking to *anyone* regarding this until the thing is settled. Let's just wait and pray and see what happens." His property being adjacent to our dairy—and twice the size with room for expansion—looked like an answer to our prayer, but not the one we were expecting. We were both kind of shell-shocked! In this county, farms remained in families for generations. It's highly unusual for them to come up for sale, and this one was so conveniently located *next door*. This had to be God orchestrating the events. We went home to discuss the huge changes that were about to affect our lives… and to pray.

Tuesday, August 17, 1998

Lord God. Father! Are You bringing to pass this next step for us? This farm? Are You really causing this to come to pass? Give Arlin courage and peace and help me to be all I need to be to help him do what You have called him to do. Only You, Lord, know what You have for him.

Arlin told me the next morning he believed God had given him a number, a price to offer. If Sam agreed, that was confirmation to move forward. They agreed on the figure, and Sam and Arlin had a deal in less than a week. Farm deals like this usually take at least six months to process and work out. Closing would be within two months.

The reason for Sam's unexpected offer? The *same* day when Arlin half jokingly said, "Hey, if you're ever interested in selling your dairy, let me know," Sam's son came home with an unexpected announcement for his father. Sam Jr. was quitting the dairy business and going to Bible school. Sam then went to his remaining three sons and asked if any of them were interested in taking over the dairy someday. Surprisingly, they all said no. If his boys weren't interested, there was no point in continuing on with the farm. In the world of dairy farming, this was about as close to a miracle as you could get.

I was shaking in my boots, wondering what all this would mean for us. Okay, I'll be honest. I was wondering what in the world this would mean for me! I already had lots of responsibilities with our current dairy. My day was more than full even though the size of our business was relatively small. Purchasing the extra farm would mean tripling our current cow numbers, and it didn't take a mathematician to figure out what that would mean: *triple* the amount of work!

Arlin took me over to see the farm. It was not in the best of shape. In fact, everywhere we looked, all I could see was work, work, and more work! But everywhere Arlin looked, all he could see was possibilities, possibilities, and more possibilities. That's one of the basic differences between Arlin and me. He's a visionary; it's part of his makeup to see potential growth and profitability. I'm the practical one, sizing things up and seeing them as black or white. I'm definitely not the risk-taker.

"Arlin," I said, "you've got to be kidding me! Do you see all the work it's going to take to make this thing go?!" I desperately tried to sound legitimately concerned rather than scared out of my mind. And that was no small task because I also had to sign my name to all those notes...those giant notes!

The most money I had ever borrowed was for a car, and that was back in 1983. I paid it off a year early. This farm thing was more than a stretch for me; this was way out of my league. This took blind faith and was just plain scary.

But, I succumbed to Arlin's excitement and felt a hint of exhilaration on my own part. I mean, this was challenging and adventurous, and the entrepreneurial part of my brain perked up. This was the most energized I had felt in a long time. Even though I was petrified of how this might all turn out, I dove into this farm venture with Arlin head first.

When it came time to name the farm, I knew immediately what we would call it. Arlin used to joke that if we ever bought our own farm we would name it "Yippee! Farms"—because whenever a new calf was born, I would cry out "Yippee!" New calves meant the herd was growing. And, whenever it rained I would also exuberantly yell, "Yippee!" because that meant the crops were growing. These were good things; I learned that early. Arlin would laugh and say that "Yippee" would be our farm name someday. He was kidding, of course.

But I held him to it. Not without flack from his family, however. In fact, one brother came over to the farm one day and said, "Deborah, I'm not afraid to tell you to your face that that is the stupidest name I ever heard. I am so embarrassed to have a brother who would name his farm that."

"Hey," I told him, "you're entitled to your opinion, but the name stays." I just shook my head and walked away, as the smile across my face got bigger and bigger.

Chapter 30

Expanding Our Territory

Thursday, October 1, 1998

Father, we own this farm as of today! You worked this out. I need to write down one day how this all came about…

On October 1st, the farm was officially ours and the work began. Man, did it begin! For the next two months, I felt like I permanently had a weed-eater attached to my hips. There were weeds four and five feet tall surrounding every structure. While I was on weed-eating duty, Arlin tore down, built, fixed, and modified. Soon the place started looking workable. The end, though, seemed nowhere in sight. Thank God for our employees at the time who worked diligently alongside us. Otherwise, we would never have seen the light of day.

By October 22, I was already crying out to God in my journals for help. *Help! Lighten the load! We need help!* The calves immediately tripled, and we built more calf barns. Translation: more feed to mix and deliver, more bedding, caretaking, vet work, *everything* times three. With the new farm came the need for a few other farms to rent for either cropland or barns, to house more animals. And I continued doing all the bookkeeping, another full-time job in and of itself.

Next to be put on my list of duties was the milking schedule. I had two parlors to schedule, each requiring a crew for three milkings a day. *Nobody* wanted the scheduling job-I tried giving it away, ordering it away to no avail, and finally accepted that it was mine. To find enough milkers to fill these two schedules was just short of a nightmare. It takes a special person to milk cows. Finding the right people became a monumental challenge. It was my second "full-time" job.

When it came to feeding *ourselves*, if it wasn't a sandwich, Arlin and I didn't recognize it. For the next four months, we'd sit in his truck outside the mini-mart at about 8 o'clock at night in our grimy farm clothes, with cow poop and dirt from head to toe, hair matted and smelling to high heaven, while eating a sandwich and drinking coffee. We'd look at each other and say, "Is this our life? Eating in a truck on a Friday night outside the mini-mart?" Then we'd look at each other again and laugh! Hey, at least we were still laughing.

I started working with our veterinarians more closely. In fact, I felt like I was becoming a herdswoman. It was an inside joke between Arlin and me. When we first got married and the herdsman at the time decided to move to Egypt, Arlin said, "You'd make a great herdsperson, honey. Didn't you always want to be a herdswoman?" Oh right. *That* was my dream. His comment didn't warrant a response, but God? Oh He had a plan, all right!

My background came in handy. I was pre-med in undergraduate school, grew up in a doctor's home, and managed a plastic surgeon's business my first two years in New York. I had gained lots of medical knowledge over the years—and I didn't even realize it until I started taking care of cows. Caring for their medical and dietary needs became my full-time occupation.

This complete immersion into the wonderful world of dairy farming and my veterinarian apprenticeship created a vertical learning curve that never seemed to level off. I was overwhelmed in the beginning, but my firsthand experience grew exponentially after we purchased Yippee! Farms.

We now had over ten silos, a gazillion conveyors and motors that meant many hundreds of tiny—never mind *giant*—things that could (and did) go wrong on a daily basis. Imagine the job description for just the maintenance manager—who, of course, was Arlin.

In all of this, I was beginning to expect the unexpected. But one thing I didn't count on was a truly unexpected blessing. I saw the Word of God come to life in a whole new way. Much of the Bible was written to an agrarian society and many of the terms refer to farming. Now having experienced farming in real life, I was seeing what I had been reading all these years, right here on our farm!

For instance, God speaks of the tilling of the hard heart and opening it up to plant seed—the seed of the Word of God—as a painful process. I struggled to imagine this in my mind. Tilling the heart? I understand what tilling means, but I often wondered about the analogy to the heart. I know when God works on my heart it's often painful; I understood that part. Then one day while I was sitting next to Arlin on the tractor, watching the ground being dug up behind us by a large ripper that had big steel hooks with sharp points, I understood. If that hard ground had nerves running through it, boy would that hurt... Imagine the emotional equivalent of those huge steel curved hooks *ripping* at the surface of your heart! But the ground had to be tilled to open up and unearth the soft soil to plant the corn seed. Otherwise, the seed wouldn't be able to grow. The hard clay-like ground wouldn't allow the seed to germinate and take root. Suddenly, God's perfect analogy came to light. By George, I think I got it!

Chapter 31

From Pennsylvania to Paris

That December, we had an opportunity to travel to Europe for 12 days. But how could we leave this new farm just three months after we purchased it, with all the work that had to be done and all the possible things that could go wrong? We didn't spend our days wondering if something would break down, just *when* it would break down, because something always did. Most of the time, Arlin ran from repair job to repair job, up and down 100-foot silos, into feed mixers, across conveyors, barns, meadow fences, and so on.

But we needed a break and no matter what, we were determined to take one. We stood fast, remained brave, and I was insistent that we go away. We rarely got away together, and I was determined that we do this. I just knew it would be the trip of a lifetime for Arlin, because he had never experienced Europe. So we scheduled everything that had to be done daily on the farms while we were gone and who would be responsible for what…and then we prayed!

We had free tickets left over from the canceled honeymoon, and places to stay with friends in Paris and Alsace. I had never been to Alsace, the eastern most region of France that borders on Germany and Switzerland. From Alsace came the tradition of the Christmas tree. I always wanted to go during the Christmas season and partake of all the street festivities, fairs, and traditional celebrations.

We arrived in Paris and were greeted by a friend I knew from New York, now living in Paris. He took us to his home just outside the city. The next day, we took the train into town and I immediately headed for Notre Dame. I was so excited as I led Arlin along at breakneck speed, talking until I was out of breath, describing all the wonders of Paris. I felt like the old me again! Here we were in Europe at Christmastime, experiencing this wonderful culture during a marvelous holiday season. I couldn't have asked for more. The decorations stretching along the Champs Elysées were spectacular! And the Seine! Oh my, so beautiful! Along the way, I pointed out some of my old stomping grounds to Arlin places where I'd stayed, cafés I'd frequented, walking paths I'd taken for early morning exercise when I visited Paris years before.

When I was single and living in New York City, my friend Linda and I used to race-walk several times a week at 6 a.m. in Central Park, alongside an interesting array of people—an eclectic group of artists, lawyers, actors, hotel managers, mothers, and writers, to name a few. On one of our walks, we met a woman named Giselle. She was from Paris, and the three of us became regular early morning walking buddies. When Giselle moved back to Paris to take a law position, she insisted that if we were ever in Paris, we were to stay with her. Linda and I took her up on her offer, and we visited her.

Giselle had an absolutely adorable place not far from the cathedral. Linda stayed with her and I rented a room across the little cobblestone driveway in a small but very charming hotel. Coincidentally, my friend Jean was going to be in Paris at the same time, to research a project for her architectural firm, so we arranged to stay together. The arrangement was wonderful; the four of us partnered to make dinners, sightsee or just visit the local cafés, but we also had our own space to retreat to, after a full day of exploring.

Linda and I mapped out a walking path that took us around Notre Dame in the wee hours every morning. We ended our energetic walks at our favorite café and sat outside sipping lattes. It was so beautiful at that time of the morning! Often a light fog would roll in, the ground a bit damp with dew, not yet warmed by the morning sun. We would bundle up in our sweatshirts and head out, chatting a million words a minute while taking in the rich surroundings; waving to the bread deliverymen, and smelling the freshly brewed coffee among the cafes. The café latte after our walk was our "carrot" to get the job done! Our walks gave me the lay of the land, and were the reason why, when Arlin and I came to Paris, I could be his guide.

Arlin and I arrived at Notre Dame shortly before lunch, and I enthusiastically pontificated about the history of the cathedral and its architecture, noting the flying buttresses, the Gothic structure, the massive front doors and their details. As I continued my monologue about the artwork and the craftsmanship, Arlin interrupted with, "It's *dark* in here!" My passion and my knowledge of the city and its wonderful enchantments were lost on Arlin; he was bored from the moment our plane landed.

We went to see Leonardo da Vinci's *Mona Lisa* at the Louvre, and we raced through in about 15 minutes. Needless to say, the Louvre generally requires a minimum of one week's time to just browse—we practically ran through it to find The *Mona Lisa.* Then, standing before her, Arlin asked, "That's it?" Okay. Now I was undone. I guess John Deere and snowmobiling for some, Europe and its painters for others. To each his own, I mused. We came home two days early. And that was that.

Chapter 32

We Need a Sign

I was chomping at the bit for spring to come. Working outside all winter long in often sub-zero temperatures, snow, sleet, and wet rain was appalling at times. One night that winter, we were called out of bed at about one in the morning because the conveyor that ran feed out to the low group of cows at Yippee! Farm wasn't working. We had to get the feed out to those cows—and pronto!

As we raced down to the farm, I had no idea what I was in for. In fact, why was I going along at all? I couldn't possibly help. But as it turned out, I was absolutely there for a reason. Because of my size and weight, Arlin had me crawl up on the feed bunk, balance myself on the end corner, and reach my arms up to hand operate the pulley. The pulley then activated the chain that ran the conveyor which deposited feed out to the feed bunk. I had to repeat this action one hand over the other as Arlin ran the feed out of the mixer onto the conveyor. Meanwhile, it was freezing! I could barely feel my arms. I thought for sure my hands were frostbitten.

Every five minutes, I had to keep yelling, *"Break!"* Then I would drop my arms and rest them.

Hey, buddy, remember me; the girl from New York with the fluffy pink slippers and the apartment off Fifth Avenue? Do you really expect me to do this?! I screamed silently to myself. Even if I were to bellow out this subtle complaint, no one would hear me, except the cows and Arlin. And let's face it; neither Arlin nor the girls would be sympathetic!

This was one of those times where I thought, "Okay God. Did I hear You right on this one? Are You *sure* this is what You had in mind for me?!" I really was becoming a farmer, and *fast!*

In the midst of all the more pressing tasks, we still hadn't had a sign made for the new farm. We had just recently decided on a scripture to go along with our logo. It was perfect. I wanted a verse from the Old Testament, so it wouldn't offend my Jewish friends. I also wanted something that was meaningful to our farm and our situation, something specific to our business. And it was God's sweet gift how the scripture came to me.

The previous Memorial Day, we went to Washington, Virginia—often referred to as "Little Washington," as many presidents have stayed there. I had always wanted to visit the Inn at Little Washington. It's just a couple hours drive west of D.C. Unfortunately, the Inn was sold out, so we ended up at another beautiful B & B just down the road from the Inn. It was built in the Federal style and had enchanting rooms. A beautiful staircase ran down the center of the house and ended near the parlor where they served afternoon tea and cookies on silver trays with bone china. My scene, totally!

After walking through the small, quaint little town that morning, we came back for a nap. I prayed before I fell asleep that God would give me a Scripture for our farm. About an hour later, I woke up and heard, "Malachi 4:2." *Okay. What does that mean and what does it say?* I grabbed my Bible on the nightstand, turned to Malachi, and read this: "But for you who revere my name, the Son of righteousness will rise with healing in his wings. And you will go out and leap like calves released from the stall." *Amazing!*

Watching the calves skipping, leaping, and jumping all over the place in ecstatic jubilation at having been released from their little stalls at the end of eight weeks had become one of my great joys. From the time a calf is born and comes to me for care, it is kept in an individual stall to protect it from catching or spreading any sickness to another calf while they are still so vulnerable. The calf remains in its stall for eight weeks until weaned from milk to whole grain and hay. At this point they're moved to a barn where nine of them, now together, learn to share their feed, water, and hay, and enjoy more space.

Whenever the time came to round up a new group of eight-week-olds, I asked the guys to radio me so I could assist and watch. We'd load them one by one on the cattle trailer and drive them to their new home. As they unloaded off the back of the trailer, not sure of where they were going, they'd step out onto the ground, albeit a little hesitantly, sniff it, and take off running, skipping, leaping, and kicking up their little back heels everywhere! I would love watching them! And just think—God knows all along about His animals and how they behave. Imagine! It blows my mind... Of *course* He knows... and wrote about it in Malachi 4:2!

Arlin agreed the scripture was perfect for the Yippee! Farms sign. So now I had a mission. Who was going to make this sign for us and what would it look like? I hired a friend from church who was a commercial artist. He created my design and off it went to the sign company. I gave him the layout, the color scheme, and the jacquard check I wanted to go with it. "That looks like a taxi cab!" he exclaimed. But, I would not be deterred. After a few persuasive conversations, I had a logo.

I hit the jackpot with the first sign maker I contacted. He was local, went to school with Arlin, and, after looking at the logo, he said, "Hey, I'll underbid any other sign company out there. I just want to do this sign for you. This is special." That sounded pretty good to me!

So, within a week I had a sign. My neighbor 'Wild Bill," who scared me to death that morning with the army fatigues and chair strapped to his back, is a wonderful carpenter, and he made the posts to mount the sign in front of the farm. Everything was ready to go, except the sign itself, which sat in Bill's basement for approximately six months because Arlin was still worried about what neighboring farmers would think. The teasing about our farm's name never ceased. That sign was pretty big too, so no one could drive by without noticing it. Arlin was thinking one foot by one foot, low to the ground, with lots of large shrubbery all around it. Designing this sign, however, was one of my few, and I mean very few, creative outlets. And, did I mention I'm from Texas? The size of the sign turned out to be around 3 ½ feet tall by 3 feet wide. That sign was going up!

One cold day in December, I was having a particularly dark day. I was tired and felt there was little tangible reward for the endless monotony of work. In sheer desperation for emotional stimulation, I called Bill and said, "Yank out that sign! We're puttin' her up today!" So, we did. He brought it over on the trailer pulled by his truck. And in the dead of winter, Wild Bill dug the holes, and up she went. I loved it! His wife came by and immediately took a photo of me standing next to it in my lovely high-fashion sub-zero coveralls; a small feat, considering the many spirited discussions with Arlin to get this thing up. Lord, it's only a sign for heaven's sake!

Yippee! Farms was official. Now delivery men hauling all kinds of feed, supplies, and equipment wouldn't end up halfway out of town wondering where the heck this "Yippee! Farms" place was. You couldn't miss the "Bigger-n-Dallas" sign. That was a good thing, because we were about to triple in size!

Chapter 33

Three Dairies?!

Over the Christmas holiday, Arlin learned that our neighbor, who milked 200 cows, was going out of business. His meadows and property were adjacent to our first dairy. When Arlin shared this with me, I wanted to pretend as if I hadn't heard this and was hoping Arlin wasn't thinking what I knew he was probably thinking. Please, no more work!

But, the next thing I knew, Arlin came to me and asked if I thought we should rent the farm. "Should we go for it or not?" he asked. That would mean *three* dairies! Take the never-ending lists of chores and duties and multiply them by three. What would that mean? *Ding, ding, ding!* More work! How exciting… When do we start?

As much as I didn't want another dairy, I encouraged him to do it. I had been praying since we first heard the rumor that our neighbor might be going out of business. I knew this might be a possibility, so I started asking the "Boss Man" early. I had peace that this was the right decision.

Wednesday, January 12, 2000

Psalm 138:8: "The Lord will fulfill his purpose for me; your love, O Lord, endures forever. Do not abandon the works of your hands."

Arlin made the deal, and the third dairy became ours to rent. This dairy was in wonderful shape. The owners kept the grounds immaculate, which excited me because my thinking was, "No projects! Yeah!" Not so. Unbeknownst to me, Arlin had been sizing up the situation. To do what? Modernize, consolidate, and create efficiencies! Okay. So that's his thing, but the work… I was freaking out just a tad. Remember, he's the visionary and I'm the practical one.

I was stretching *way* past my limit. This felt more like diving off a cliff, hoping someone would be holding a net at the bottom to catch me. Arlin brought in about 80 bred heifers so we could begin milking at the third Yippee! location. Now I had three milking schedules to fill. Again, no one on the farm wanted the job of scheduling, so I still hadn't been able to delegate it! Arlin's encouragement to me was, "Deborah, you have to be willing to do whatever it takes to make this thing work. You can't just do the things you want to do." Well, I kept waiting for the *singular* thing I liked to do to come along, never mind the *things* (plural) I liked to do. *Get real, Arlin!*

My saving grace was God's wondrous creation, this marvelous place where we lived and worked, and all its amazing beauty. The calves had become my refuge since I was infertile and the cows my hope for new life and a future.

I prayed and sang to my baby calves daily as I fed them and worked with them. I would frequent the barns, walking through and around them praying over the cows for protection, health, physical comfort, and contentment with us at Yippee! Farms. A happy cow makes for a lot of happy milk! That meant the cows—their well-being and comfort—were *numero uno* on the farm. If those girls were lying down chewing their cud all relaxed and pleased, then we were pleased!

Chapter 34

Kittens of Glory

As spring faithfully arrived, so did the 300 daffodils and tulips I had planted the year before. Bulbs were my most recent discovery in nature, and my current reason for smiling. To look at those gorgeous flowers popping up all over the place—I couldn't quite remember where I had put them last fall—was a glorious sight to behold. How did God think these things up? Bulbs planted about 3 inches into the ground in the fall come up in the spring all by themselves year after year. "Gotta give it to You, God, You're pretty creative..."

Summer, fall, and winter were all pretty much the same as far as the farm was concerned. Work, work, and more work. I became very aware of this one day as I walked into the jewelry store one day during the summer to drop off my watch for repairs. My friend Randy, who owned the shop said, "How's it going Deborah?"

I sighed. "Well, I just wish there were about twelve more hours of light in each day. Just don't have enough time to get it all done."

"Yep," he said, "I can tell you've become a farmer. Only farmers ask for longer days." That was a newsflash for me; I really didn't think I had taken on a posture of ownership. All I knew was that I just needed more time every day to get the chores done. But something was definitely feeling more at home in the role of "farmer."

Even though the workload was massive day in and day out, God allowed for respites of the heart every now and then. One of mine was spring's gift of kittens! I quickly learned that every spring and summer, lots and lots of kittens arrive. All the barn cats get pregnant and have one or two litters each. A kitten has to be one of God's cutest creations. Then again, most baby animals are just too cute to resist.

To witness God's glory was to find where the cats hid their litters. Our herdsman, depending upon whether he enjoyed the kittens himself, would usually stumble upon a litter or two in the barn feed room, a silo, a barn wall, a feed trough, under a bush—almost anywhere!

One morning our tractor guy called me out to the shop and said, "Deborah, come here and open this tool drawer." As I opened it, I saw a litter of five kittens! How she managed to crawl up in that drawer and have her babies I don't know. It was adorable seeing her lying there with those five kittens all sucking on her. Their little paws, when they're sucking, push against the momma cat like they're kneading her tummy. It's such a small wonder, but one that reminds me there is a Creator in heaven who thought up this detail, and I'm privileged to experience it with joy.

Another day during feeding, one of the farmhands radioed that a heifer had gotten herself stuck during the night in the feed trough. That meant she may have been without feed or water for up to 24 hours. I rushed over there immediately to see what we needed to do. By the time I arrived, a couple of the guys had already pulled her out, but she was weak and dehydrated. I felt horrible for her, but freak accidents do happen. The heifers are curious, and they often go poking around and occasionally end up in a predicament.

I raced back to the home farm to get grain and a five-gallon bucket of water. When I returned within fifteen minutes, I found the most endearing scene I could ever imagine. There was the heifer, lying down with a kitten asleep under her head! The two of them looked so sweet together! And since the kitten was all wet, I could tell the heifer had been licking her. *Isn't that just like God to send a kitten to keep her company while she recuperates!*

Arlin doesn't quite have the fascination with the kittens that I do. Generally speaking, neither do most of the farmhands. But I find that when I look into their tiny faces, I just have to smile. How can anyone resist a kitten? My daily fix, spring and summer, became finding a litter, bringing them milk if they were old enough, and just holding one or two of them. This was cheap therapy as far as I was concerned! Whenever things got tough on the farm and I was feeling down, discouraged, or overwhelmed, the antidote was to find a kitten and forget about everything else for a few moments. I could go the denial route, but escapism was the obvious choice because more often than not, when I left the kittens, I had a lighter mood and a little more hope.

It all sounds so trite and ridiculous, but most of us live the majority of our lives Sunday through Saturday, racing from one task to the next. We start all over again on Sunday finding ourselves easily caught in a weekly, cyclical rut. There are mountaintop experiences of course, but those are the exceptions. As I see it, I have to be alert and look all around me, every day, to see small surprises—glimpses of God's glory. I need to see manifestations of Him, of His power and majesty, to stay alive and vibrant. And I do find them, at least one every single day, without fail, and sometimes in the tiny face of a kitten.

I also remember a different kind of revelation right after we purchased the third dairy. I was out having coffee with my friend Grace when we bumped into one of her friends. When Grace introduced us, I said, "Hello, I'm Deborah Benner. I'm a Dairy Farmer."

Grace's eyes got big and she coughed out a laugh, "Deborah, did you just hear yourself, what you just said?"

"Uh… all I did was introduce myself; what's the big deal?"

Grace kept smiling, "You've never introduced yourself as a dairy farmer. You've always said, 'I'm married to a dairy farmer.' Do you realize the transformation that's taken place? Oh my God! You've actually *become* a dairy farmer!"

She was right. I was no longer saying, "I'm *married* to a dairy farmer," making it very clear that it was not my occupation. Now I was saying, "Hi, I *am* a dairy farmer." And therein lays the power of God. Before I knew it, I was stating the truth about who I was with a sense of ownership and pride, no longer disillusioned about the reality of my life. But it didn't stop there. I was about to delve even deeper into the world of dairy; not just my own, but into the inner workings of the aggregate farming community around me. It is through my subsequent ventures that I was dubbed "The Dairy Queen."

PART FOUR

NO GOING BACK

"...who knows maybe you were made Queen for just such a time as this"
(The Message, Eugene Peterson)

Chapter 35

Show Me the Money

To him be glory and power forever and ever! Amen. (Revelation 1:6)
After I began managing the books for our dairy business, one of the first things I discovered about the check we received for our milk was that there was a big part missing! Where was it going?

I asked Arlin, "What is this large deduction that is taken out of our milk check and who authorizes it?"

"Oh, that goes to the check-off and the government dues," he answered.

"The what and the who?"

"The dairy check-off, you know those commercials you see about milk, the milk mustache, and the 'got milk' ads? That's where the money goes. Ten cents per hundred weight of milk shipped gets taken out automatically and sent to check-off. It's a commodities program the government supports."

"Oh...you mean we're paying for advertising?"

"Basically, that's what it is," he said.

"Well, wait a minute. You mean I have this much money automatically deducted from my check and I don't get a say in how it's spent?"

"I really don't know much about it, Deborah. I don't have time to worry about it. They take the money out and that's about all I know."

They take money out without asking us?!

"Arlin, I think we should have a say in how this money is spent. I mean look at the latest ad. There's a superstar model with a milk mustache. Do you think anyone believes she drinks milk? I lived in New York; I know the scene. Some of them battle eating disorders for Pete's sake, and they definitely don't do dairy. Why aren't they using star athletes who are healthy and need energy and nutrition? That would be more believable to me, not some "pick-thin" super model!"

"What do you know about advertising, Deborah? You have enough to do already. Just leave it to the experts," he said, dismissively.

Just the push I needed. *Humph! Leave it to the experts! This is our business; it's our money! Doesn't that at least give us a say?*

Besides, I did have a bit of a background in advertising. Back in Texas, I worked for the largest family-owned advertising agency as an assistant account executive. One of my accounts was the agency's largest national account. I was on the ad team for two years. I wasn't an ad genius, but I had experience.

The next day, I started making phone calls. I didn't find out much. But I was not about to let that deter me. Next, I made a visit to the co-op that ships our milk. No surprise: I was pretty forthright with my questions. I wanted to know how much money they got and who was deciding how to spend it! Plus, I wanted to know how I could get a say in this whole thing. It was, after all, our money too.

I didn't get too far there, either. No one seemed interested in talking and even if they were, I got the sense that they weren't about to share any "inside info" with the pushy, loud-mouthed Italian. For one reason or another— maybe the other million urgent things on my daily "to do" list—I gave up pretty quickly and accepted it. My plate was already full. This mystery, however, continued to gnaw at me, way back in the recesses of my mind.

Then, one day while en route to drop the mail at the trailer, I noticed the quarterly mailing about milk. Out of curiosity, I picked it up. My eyes skimmed over the first page until I reached the bottom. There I saw an announcement that someone's term on the dairy board was expiring and they were taking nominations. I read on, and there in black in white was my answer to who gets a say in how our advertising money is spent. The members of the Dairy Board are the spokespeople for the farmers! They decide how to spend dairy farmers' money on advertising. *Hmm… How do you get on this thing?*

I looked around the page for a phone number. I called six different numbers before I was finally given a number with a 202 area code. I called. It was the Secretary of Agriculture's office in Washington D.C.

"Hi, Eleanor? My name is Deborah Benner and I just received this mailing announcing that someone is retiring from this board and that you're accepting nominations for the position. Is that correct?"

"That's right," she replied.

"Oh, I see. Well, how do you get on this board?"

"Well, first, you have to be a dairy farmer with a working dairy," she began.

"Okay, I qualify so far," I said quickly.

"Then, you have to be nominated."

"I see." *Pause.* "Well, who has to nominate you?" I probed further.

"Cattle registry associations, your federal and state legislators, or any other leaders in the dairy industry or government," she said.

"Oh, okay." I quickly ran through my list of the aforementioned to see whom I might know. I came up with zero.

"Can I nominate myself?" I inquired. There seemed to be a small snicker on the other end of the phone...

"I guess you could, but the applications are due May 31, and that's tomorrow." I believe she was a little dumbfounded by my persistence, especially since I didn't seem to know much about the proper procedures.

"Well, I have a fax machine. Do you?" I asked.

Pause. "Of course," she said.

"Well, then, can you fax me the application? I'll give you my number."

"Okay, but you have to have it in by tomorrow, so hurry," she urged, then thanked me for calling and hung up.

My first realization; government procedures can often be complicated. Hence, I received this enormous fax. I don't know what I thought I'd receive—perhaps a one or two page application, but definitely not this 20-page document! I wondered how long it would take to fill out. I had to get back down to the farm—I hadn't even taken my boots off!

Regardless, I sat down and started writing. I quickly made copies of my business resume and then my acting resume. I put it all together in about an hour and faxed it right back, then sent the hard copies via Federal Express... and then I forgot about it. I told Arlin I had just nominated myself to be on the committee or board or something because I knew they had a hand in spending our advertising money and I wanted a say.

"That's nice, honey," he said, and kept on doing what he was doing. I figured what I just said fell outside his radar zone and didn't even register. Oh well. He probably thought it was just another one of his wife's pet projects—as if I needed more to do.

That was at the end of May, just shortly after we returned from Texas and the failed IVF procedure. June arrived and the whole episode of adopting the Russian children was just beginning. I was way too preoccupied with the adoptions to give the "board thing" another thought.

At the end of June, I received another mailer. I quickly read it and ran back down to the farm to find Arlin and show him what it said.

"Honey, I just got this newsletter that announced this other lady got that position I nominated myself for. I'm a little bummed, but oh well. It wasn't God's will. It's not like I've got nothing to do and all this time on my hands anyway, right?"

"Let me see that." He took the paperwork from my hand and read it over. He began shaking his head and smiling, eyebrow raised, "Honey," he replied, "that lady got a local-level position. You must have applied for a position on the *national* level."

"Really?" I said with incredulity…and a little hope. I didn't even know when or how to find out if my nomination was accepted. I assumed I would get a letter if, by chance, my nomination did get accepted and what the next steps would be. I imagined there would be a voting process or something. It was a long shot, anyway, so I basically forgot about it once again.

As the leaves began to change, the magnificent month of October was ushered in with all its color and glory, and cooler weather. Harvest season was one of the most rewarding times on the farm. You get to see firsthand the fruits of your labor. Silos are filled and there's a deep feeling of satisfaction. I was on my daily run back to the house to drop off the mail, when I heard the answering machine beeping. The fourth message was from the Secretary of Agriculture's office in Washington D.C. "I'm looking for Deborah Benner," the male voice said. "Could you please have her call me at the following number?"

"I wonder if that's another one of those agricultural census calls when they ask you a million stats about your animals, crops, land, milk production, and so on. I don't have time to call him back. I'll do it tomorrow." I thought to myself.

As I started back out the door, the phone rang. Thankful for caller ID, I saw it was the Secretary of Agriculture's office calling again. Curious, I answered. After I confirmed that I was indeed Deborah Benner, the caller said, "Hi, Deborah. I'm Richard Kopp, and I'm calling you today to let you know that you have been appointed to the National Dairy Board. That is, if you'll accept the position."

"I've been appointed? Oh! Well…yes, sure. Okay, I accept," I said not knowing exactly what it was I had agreed to.

"You'll be formally inducted at the meeting in Florida. You are planning on attending, aren't you?"

Now I really felt ridiculous. What meeting? I had no idea what he was referring to. Anyone who had reached this level of board status had been serving on other levels of promotion boards. They attended these meetings and were well aware of the annual meeting to which he referred. Again, in my ignorance, I scrambled to say something.

"Yes, of course I'll be there. Could you please just remind me of when that is, again?"

"In November. You'll be receiving a whole packet of information in the mail with all the details. Well, congratulations, and we'll see you in Florida," he said and hung up.

I sat for a few moments, stunned...... The National Dairy Board! Quickly, I jumped on the Internet to look up the Secretary of Agriculture and the National Dairy Board to find out what I had just committed myself to, all the while wondering if my husband was going to kill me! I was just trying to get a "say" in how our money is spent... really!

I printed out everything I could find and hurried back down to the farm. "Arlin, honey, look, I got it! I got this appointment to the National Dairy Board; you know the one that spends those check-off dollars we send in for advertising? Look right here and read what I'm supposed to do," I blurted out as we both began reading. We still didn't know what this would involve or what implications it might have concerning the farm; he was as shocked as I was. But I could tell he was proud, and I was feeling a slight bit vindicated over our seven-year argument regarding having input into the dairy advertising. Guess what? I was just about to have input – on a national level!

Chapter 36

The Dairy Queen

The November meeting was here before we knew it. Arlin and I took off for my first annual American Dairy Promotion meeting in Orlando, Florida. I was a little nervous to fly because it was November 2001, following September 11th. The nation was still in major recovery mode. It was a little surreal; being in Orlando, our hotel on the Disney property. You could throw a bowling ball down any of the streets on the property; there were no cars, no traffic, and no lines for the rides. But, the meeting was on and everyone was humming away with activity in the conference area.

It was a gorgeous hotel on a beautiful property. Our room was magnificent. What a major retreat from our 1976 model single-wide! I could actually step out of the shower while Arlin brushed his teeth, without running into each other!

As I walked through the hotel lobby to the conference room, I was filled with excitement and anticipation. As I approached the growing crowd of mostly men, they greeted each other like old friends, patting each other on the back, hugging, and acting like they had known each other for years. I was the new *girl* on the block. No one greeted me; no one knew who I was. They probably thought I was hotel staff, there to oversee the catered brunch or something. Several hundred dairy farmers from all over the nation were in attendance, representing different state and local board members as well as the 33 National Dairy Board members. "This is some big meeting," I thought to myself.

Once they realized I was actually there to attend the meeting, the focus was uncomfortably on me. It didn't take long to hear the whispers, "Who is she? Who recommended her? Who nominated her?" I could almost hear their inner dialogue, "What has she done, who does she know?"

Soon after, I had my introduction to the staff. I was put on the audit committee right off the bat. This was unusual for a newly appointed member because the job was to go over the finances with a fine-toothed comb and was usually given to members with a few more years of experience. But it was a tedious job and one not envied, so I was the one assigned to the task. This was exactly what I wanted, so I could get the 'dollars and sense' of things. I had a lot to say about how our money was being spent and I said it, loud and clear. As the staff wondered who I was and how in the world I got this position, I became ever more insistent and vocal about my belief that all dairy farmers had the same motto; "all for one and one for all." True, depending on which camp you were in, especially *which male* camp you were in. I was very naïve, to say the least.

Another newly appointed committee member, James Freed, befriended me and took the time to understand where I was coming from and that my intentions were to better spend our advertising dollars. He spoke up and said, "Hey, this lady has advertising agency experience, she's not just a dairy farmer; she knows what she's talking about, you'd better listen to her!" Thanks for speaking up for me buddy, but I have a feeling it might hit you from behind later on!

My husband had cautioned me, "Deborah, just keep your mouth shut and listen. Don't make any waves." (Moi make waves???) But in keeping with my nature, I called it like I saw it and became "the one in the lunch room no one wanted to sit next to." Welcome to politics 101. I had walked into a crash course!

But something interesting happened in my district with my local farming community. As a result of my appointment to the National Dairy Board, I began to receive calls from local agricultural boards asking me to sit on their boards and committees. I guess they figured the loud-mouthed farmer gal might be good for something, after all!

An entirely new chapter in my life had just begun. I was elected and appointed to serve on an array of local and national agricultural boards and hence the reason for my new title among family and friends: The Dairy Queen! My commitments were growing. In addition to my board and farm work, I was serving on more committees and local advocacy groups for land development, even the manure management task force! For a short time I was the "manure queen." I made sure that title got dropped fast, but I have to laugh to think how I started in this community as this actress from New York City with the mouth.

A brand new world had just opened up. It was another vertical learning curve, only this time I was dealing with the challenges facing the agricultural industry on every level; local, state and national. I was acquiring a wealth of knowledge of the political difficulties, regulations, and American agricultural philosophies and their implications on the future of farming in America. It's a fight on every front. This allowed me to network with farmers across the country, which in turn increased my knowledge and educational resources exponentially! At the suggestion of my industry peers, I began reading every trade paper, magazine, and newsletter I could get my hands on. My business experience from the past jumped front and center, and I was on a mission to get educated and make a difference. Naïve perhaps, but again I had no clue. This new journey into the world of politics and farming was unlike any other I had experienced.

It was simultaneously exciting, exhilarating, and frustrating. I loved this change of direction, the challenge to make a difference. However, as usual, in keeping with the way I'm wired, I didn't consider the magnitude of the task at hand—quite frankly I just didn't know. Ignorance is not bliss; I jumped in with both feet—and oh my, how deep this manure pit was!

At this point, I was freaking out! I didn't know what I got myself into. I started to question, "Do I need to add anymore to my plate? There's only one of me, and I just took on another full-time job."

In one of Tim Keller's sermons, my pastor in New York, he speaks about the sovereignty of God placing you in a city or neighborhood for a purpose. Tim poses the question, "Is that city or neighborhood better or improved because you moved there? Is your being there making a difference? Are people thankful that you live among them?" This was exactly the encouragement and affirmation I needed to forge ahead.

More calls and notes began coming in from individuals locally, statewide, and even nationally, for me to get involved in politics. "Deborah, you need to run for office, really, you're bold, courageous and not afraid to expose the truth. If you run, let me know, I'll be the first one to donate to your campaign." Okay, wait a minute here, we have how many cows to milk, employees to manage, a marriage to tend to, and what about those kids?

Don't get me wrong, I loved this feeling of belonging, having a purpose, and actually contributing to this community and to agriculture as a whole. But I was getting lost in the all the "causes" and began neglecting the most important relationship in my life; the one with my husband.

PART FIVE

GETTING COMFORTABLE IN THE BACKSEAT

For this reason a man will leave his father and mother and be united to his wife,
and the two will become one flesh.
(NIV Ephesians 5:31, 33)

Chapter 37

I Had Forgotten

In the midst of working on the farm, traveling for board meetings, and dealing with infertility, I realized that my relationship with Arlin was suffering. I had gotten so into the "groove" of making my way in this community and this life of agriculture, that our marriage seemed more like a "business" arrangement than a marriage. It's almost impossible when you work with your husband, to separate business from personal. And because we didn't have children to add a family dynamic, we both worked from sunrise to sunset, both managing the business and our schedules.

To make matters worse, I constantly struggled with whether Arlin or I was at the helm of our business. Of course, in God's eyes, there was never a question, Arlin was. So imagine the tension with two of us trying to run a business, Arlin giving direction to our employees and my following up behind, giving different instructions. The employees were confused, "who's the boss? We think it is Arlin, but that wife of his, oh my…" I won't say more. I was supposed to be working alongside him, not undermining his authority; it makes for a contentious situation.

We sought marriage counsel from our church leadership as the arguments about how to run the business grew intense and seemingly impossible to resolve. I kept receiving the same advice, from our pastor, the elders, my women mentors in New York and Texas, "Deborah, you have got to back off and let him lead. There can't be two bosses, you need to do your work and let him make the decisions and run the business. You need to humble yourself and let him lead! What's more important, your marriage or that business?"

My thinking was, we're not living in the 1950's here, and we are not Ozzie and Harriet! I was a businesswoman before I ditched that security for acting in New York. I can run a business, he needs me, and I WILL NOT be a doormat!" Actually, I voiced this at every meeting we had.

Sometimes I think I was on automatic pilot. Living in a rural agricultural community without children was pretty lonely for me as a woman. A woman without children in a farming community, well, they don't know what to do with you, and so they don't do anything.

I was navigating my life in a "man's" world. Most women my age had grown children or were fast becoming grandmothers, the rest were neck-high in activities with their children. They called one another and got together because their kids played soccer on the same team or played tennis together. There was a social network of moms and when you don't have kids, you're not included. It wasn't mean it just was. That's no excuse. I was contentious and insistent that I was right in the way I was handling our marriage and our business. Of course, it wasn't producing the lifelong "dream" relationship I had prayed for all those years ago. I had the "dream" guy, but the marriage part wasn't quite happening. And whose fault was it? Mine. But, I didn't see it, I really did not.

Then one day, one of our tenants invited me to weekly Bible study at her church. I didn't attend the women's Bible studies at our church because it was too far away to trot off to so early in the morning, and still get my chores done. I did, however, long to socialize with some women and create a friendship or two. Her church was only 10 minutes from the farm and I could do it, so I went.

About the second or third week into the study, I arrived in tears, having just come from a horrendous argument with Arlin about an employee situation. I knew I was right, and he was wrong... AGAIN... and that only if he could be more forceful, intentional, and confrontational—more like me— then everything would run more smoothly and improve! I was confronting him on EVERY front for Pete's sake. My work on the various boards had led me into political situations, and I become like the "town crier", waving my fist and speaking out for truth, justice, and whatever I thought was right. While it is our civic duty to hold the line and stand up for what is truthful and just, I had not been appointed to run the world, last Arlin checked, and he let me know it... often.

The leader of our small group entertained me, allowing me to explain my exasperation, and then like a gavel dropping on the judges desk she said with her arm stretched across the table and finger pointed at me, "Enough!! Deborah you are wrong! And until you repent, seek your husband's forgiveness, and allow him to lead, things will NOT go well for you in your marriage!"

Like traveling through a time warp, I suddenly saw myself back in Central Park, walking on that spectacular fall day when I was faced with my own personal "burning bush." God had asked that fateful question, "Are you ready to take a backseat? I'm ready to bring your husband, but you'll have to take a backseat, Can you do that?" At the time I had said, a resounding "Yes!" But every day of my marriage, I was saying, "No, no, no!" not only to Arlin, but to God. The truth of my fraudulent existence hit me squarely in the heart. I had accepted God's gift of a husband, but I had not kept my word; I was still fighting to be in the front seat.

God had just divided the Red Sea right in front of me. Through this Bible study leader, He just silenced me—no minor miracle! I sat there, my mouth agape, my heart nearly stopped, what could I say? Nothing. My tears dried up instantly, and I sat there embarrassed and humbled...*in front of 12 women I had just met!* Looking for a friend, anyone? I had forgotten what I had learned way back in Dale Carnegie's sales course, "Winning friends and influencing people." Needless to say, I wasn't tearing up the joint.

However, I heard Him, you know... God was LOUD AND CLEAR this time. The info wasn't new, but the source was; this woman, Beth, I had just become acquainted with, and she was His choice of delivery. The Holy Spirit had just spoken, opened my heart, and I heard. It only took 14 years, better late than never.

I went home that day completely bewildered. I didn't speak much, I just reflected on what had happened, the veil of denial having been lifted off my heart, and the truth of who I had become— who I really was, revealed. I sheepishly began to speak to God. "Really? This is what I've done? This is who I am? This is not so good, is it?" Silence.

Not long after that, I was in my mother-in-law Eileen's kitchen, where my sister-in-law Noel was making applesauce. She began bubbling over about this new book she was reading, saying how it had changed her life; and had she known the information *ten years ago,* how different her marriage would have been.

"Different *her* marriage would be?" I thought to myself. I always thought she and her husband had a nearly perfect marriage; she always seemed so submissive and easy... the perfect wife. I asked her, "What do you mean?" She explained how she realized that her husband was the leader, not her, and how she had not respected him the way she should, and on and on. When she told me the name of the book, I realized I had already been given two copies over the last few years by friends. Obviously, I had shelved them, believing I didn't need "marriage" advice on how to respect and love my husband.

I went home that afternoon and dug out the book. I'd like to say I finished reading it in one sitting. Not so. In fact, it took me the entire fall to work my way through it. God was doing an amazing transformation in my heart, and every step of the way, as He revealed my sin to me, He opened my eyes to my own deception. God showed me how I misapplied scripture in various circumstances—it wasn't like getting a tune up; it was a whole new engine!

Daily, as He gently revealed the error of my thinking, my attitudes, and my actions towards Arlin over the past 14 years, I would weep, literally, and God would most graciously assure me that I was forgiven. He was changing me. The book gave me practical things to do, to show respect to Arlin and demonstrate my love. This was so against my nature, to my Italian temperament. However, in a genuine desire to change, I began trying new things to honor Arlin.

Most unexpectedly in such a time of deep transformation and revelation, repenting truly became a joy. I had such grace, unlike anything I had ever experienced in my 30 years of knowing the Lord. I never experienced such a gift and such joy to *repent*. It was easy, actually. He made it easy. I wanted to change, I longed to prove to Arlin that I was different, that I did love him, I did respect him, and I did trust his lead.

After a month or two, people at church walked up to me and said, "Deborah, it seems like you and Arlin are really doing well." I would think to myself, first of all, I don't know this person very well and secondly, what are they seeing, exactly? Then I realized, as the Holy Spirit was changing me, Arlin was responding, and I guess the new love growing between us was becoming evident. Even the women at my Bible study began to comment on how they could see such change in me, my attitudes, and my comments about Arlin.

The holiday season came, Thanksgiving and Christmas, and they were the best we had ever spent with his family in 14 years. I had new eyes and a changed marriage.

It was amazing what I was learning… things that seemed so simple, but were so transforming in our marriage. For example I learned that men just want you to *be* with them. They don't need a romantic interlude with flowers, breakfast in bed or a candlelit dinner. They truly want their woman to just be with them doing something that they enjoy and to enjoy it with them. So, one Friday morning, Arlin called from the tractor and said, "Hey honey, let's go out for dinner tonight, let's have a date night." I was psyched, dinner away just the two of us, one of our favorite things to do, go out to a neat place for dinner. I spent the afternoon getting ready, knowing he would be home at anytime and he only needed five minutes to get ready so I wanted to be prepared.

Arlin called around 5 and said, "Hey honey… "By the tone of his voice I knew this meant no dinner date. "The fertilizer sprayer just broke down and I have to go up to Paul B's for parts. You wouldn't want to go along with me and I promise we'll go out to dinner afterward?"

Going to Paul B's, "the parts place" is quite the experience. It is mostly frequented by farmers who are Black hatters, Amish, and Mennonite, who walk in covered in grease or some type of animal manure. Most have come for the same reason; a breakdown of some sort and this is the place to get the replacement parts. This place is 45 minutes away. "Oh, and by the way, they close at 8:30pm so we need to leave NOW!"

The Deborah of eight months earlier would have said, "No, you go ahead, I'll just make myself dinner and stay home with CeCe." But, I said, "Sure," and waited for him to swing by and get me. No time to change; we jumped into his farm truck, me dressed to the nines, perfumed and with our pet CeCe, a 3-lb Yorkie Teacup and her purse carrier. CeCe is another story, a dairy farmer with an INSIDE dog that weighs three pounds and has more outfits than I do… that *in itself* was history-making in Lancaster County.

Anyway, off we went. Upon arriving, the usual host of patrons were there, either having just pulled up in their beat-up farm trucks or their horse and buggy. I stepped out of the truck dressed like I just shopped at Saks Fifth Avenue, complete with Yorkie Teacup poking her cute little head out of my purse carrier, let's just say I looked a little out of place, but, I was determined to have fun and "be with him" in his world. Arlin proceeded down the aisles looking for parts and trying to configure some contraption for his sprayer. I, on the other hand, grabbed a giant shopping cart to shop for…nothing of course, but I put CeCe's purse in the top and took her out to run around in the basket. We slowly walked up and down every aisle in that store trying to stay busy while Arlin discussed with the salesman how to put his machine together. I don't think I have to mention the looks I was getting. I giggled as I imagined what they were thinking, "What in the world is SHE doing in here and with that, that… dog!"

Thank the Lord the Amish children with their parents came over and made a fuss over CeCe, petting and holding her. That made the parents happy and tolerant of the Foo-Foo dog and her mother! It took everything in me to hold back from laughing, it was such a scene. I just smiled and kept nonchalantly cruising the aisles; perhaps I would find something to buy after all… a new tool, or maybe a hose, and a drill?? You just never know.

Afterwards, we went through the drive- thru at Burger King, something I never do. You would have thought Arlin had died and gone to heaven! He kept smiling and I could not believe how much fun I was having just being with him. I was really enjoying myself just hanging out and 'doing nothing' with my husband! I kept wondering why it took so long to do this.

Another Friday night that was particularly memorable was when Arlin was out late spraying his cornfields. CeCe and I went to bring him dinner on the tractor. As we climbed up into the cab Arlin said, "Hey honey, why don't you ride with me, come on, there's something I want to show you, it'll be fun. I promise." Old Deborah would have said, "No thanks, I have too much to do at the house. Enjoy your dinner." But the NEW me heard herself say with enthusiasm, "OK!" He pulled down the little side seat in the cab for an extra rider. CeCe and I plopped down, and off we went.

Arlin had just purchased the latest and greatest in tractor technology, a GPS system that tracks the field. "It steers the tractor for me from the satellite!" Arlin couldn't wait to show me. As he was demonstrating this marvelous new wonder, he throws up his hands and says, "Look, hands free!" He was so cute; like a kid with a new bike. And now his hands were free… That tractor drive became VERY romantic. Who would have guessed?

Chapter 38

A Thread in His Tapestry

Give thanks to the Lord for he is good and his love endures forever! (Psalm 136:1)

God, my Father, Jesus, His Son, my Savior and Holy Spirit, my Comforter, thank You that You have my days numbered and in Your hand. Thank You that You have our children numbered and in Your hands. You who set the sun, moon, and stars in their exact places, set the heavens, spread out the earth and the seas, delivered Israel from Egypt, saved Your chosen from hell and death by way of Jesus Christ, and struck down mighty kings — I give thanks to the God of heaven! God, Father, You designed such a detailed, organized world. How can people pray and say You don't care about the details? Just look at Your creation! Thank You, God, for this lovely, pleasant creation You have made. I so enjoy Your design. Bless You for this, Father God! And Jesus and Holy Spirit who helped in this!

Funny how the tapestry of life which God weaves sometimes comes into full view, while at other times I've asked, "Hey, did You weave me off the loom?!" But lately, I'm feeling a part of the very fabric that creates the beautiful picture; fully integrated with the world around me. My past experiences, good and bad, have moved me to a place of humility and thankfulness... and purpose. While I don't know what the future holds in terms of having children or political endeavors, I do know I'm thankful for the present. God gave me the 'man of my dreams.' Only, He had to mold my heart and mind to recognize, not only the man, but also the sweetness of the dreams.

God is still molding. And I am trying to remain shapeable, conforming myself to His plans for me in my marriage, my community, my industry and His kingdom.

Deborah at 5 years of age

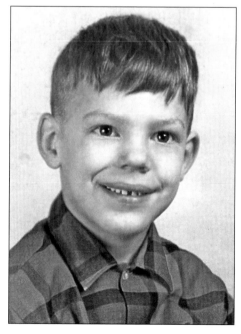

Arlin at 5 years of age

*Front door of my New York Apartment,
inspiration for my house later.*

*View walking from my New York Apartment
walking towards Central Park.*

Front of my New York Apartment

A picture of Yippee Farms!

The Heifer Barns

Arlin's trailer when we first met.

My neighborhood in New York.

Arlin's neighborhood in Lancaster.

Myself when we first met.

Arlin when we first met.

Arlin and I at Yippee Farms